wine trivia

e. michael quinlan
paul pollock
shannon quinlan

Published by Quinlan Press, Inc.
131 Beverly Street
Boston, MA 02114
(617) 227-4870

Cover design by Cathy Armstrong

Library of Congress Catalog Card Number
85-70068
ISBN 0-9611268-9-2

Photo Credits:
Kobrand Corp.
Buena Vista Vineyard
Villa Banfi

First printing April 1985
Second printing July 1985

Published by

Quinlan Press
131 Beverly Street
Boston, Massachusetts 02114

"To those who always wanted to know about wine but were afraid to ask."

Mike Quinlan

E. Michael Quinlan, a graduate of the United States Naval Academy at Annapolis, is an attorney in Boston, Massachusetts. He is the publisher of several legal periodicals, as well as *The WINE NEWSLETTER*.

Paul Pollock is a wine columnist for several newspapers and a contributor to numerous wine publications. He is currently a member of Compagnon du Beaujolais.

Shannon Quinlan, Mr. Quinlan's eldest daughter, assisted in editing and proofreading *WINE TRIVIA* and is credited with preparing the section on the wines of Spain and Portugal.

Table of Contents

ACKNOWLEDGEMENT

The authors acknowledge that in any effort such as WINE TRIVIA, a great deal of the work has already been done for them in the many scholarly and exhaustive encyclopedia that exist. Therefore, lest the reader be unduly alarmed at the depth of our knowledge, let us acknowledge some of the sources of the enclosed "Eruditia":

Alexis Lichine's "New Encyclopedia of Wines and Spirits," Third Edition; Frank Schoonmaker's "Encyclopedia of Wine," Fifth Revised Edition; "Book of California Wine" by Muscatine, Amerine and Thompson; Pauline and Sheldon Wasserman's "Guide to Fortified Wines," and Burton Anderson's "Vino."

We would also like to extend our appreciation to the public relations departments of the following companies for providing us with photographs: Buena Vista Winery, Kobrand Corporation, Villa Banfi, The Christian Brothers, Shafer Vineyards, Robert Mondavi Winery, William Hill Vineyards and Sebastiani Vineyards.

QUESTIONS

GENERAL

1. Who is credited with saying, "When one glass of wine invites the second, the wine is good"?

2. What country is the largest producer of wine?

3. What country is the largest consumer of wine?

4. What makes sparkling wine "sparkle"?

5. What is produced from distilling wine?

6. What are the four broad categories of wines?

7. What happens when white wines "maderize"?

8. What is the capacity and bottle equivalent of an imperial?

9. What is the capacity and bottle equivalent of a jeroboam?

10. What is the capacity and bottle equivalent of a magnum?

11. What is the capacity and bottle equivalent of a salmanazar?

12. What is *phylloxera,* and what is its importance?

13. What is the Latin term for the European vine most commonly used for making wine?

14. Who was the first to use a cork to seal wine in a bottle?

15. What was Dom Pérignon's principle occupation?

16. What was Dom Pérignon's handicap, which is said to have helped developed the sensitivity of his palate?

17. What is the only other country other than France where sparkling wine can legally be called Champagne?

18. What American president commented favorably on the vintage of 1784?

19. What is the British term for red Bordeaux wines?

20. What famous artist painted the image which appears on the upper half of the Château Mouton Rothschild 1973 label?

21. Who, besides the artists, signs the Château Mouton labels?

22. What is the term used for wines

named for the grapes from which they are made?

23. What is the term used for wines sold in this country which are from broad categories (such as Chablis, Burgundy, Port and Chianti)?

24. What is the ideal temperature for storing wines?

25. When storing wine, what is the result of lack of humidity?

26. When storing wine, what is the result of too much humidity?

27. What effect do standing odors have on stored wines?

28. When wines are being stored, what is the result of vibration or premature movement?

29. What is the optimum level of humidity for storing wines?

30. Very young red wines show what color at the edge of the glass?

31. Very young white wines show what color at the edge of the glass?

32. During what course of a meal would one expect to be served Château d'Yquem?

33. True/False: The greater the grape harvest the better the grape quality.

34. The method of designating the grape crop size in Europe is based on what system?

35. What is the European measure of "yield"?

36. A hectolitre is how many litres of wine?

37. A hectolitre is how many bottles of wine?

38. A hectare is how many acres of land?

39. Generally, a ton of grapes yields how many gallons of wine, or how many hectolitres per hectare?

40. How long should fast-maturing wines, including Beaujolais, rest before being opened?

41. How long should an expensive, fine red wine, sufficiently dated at purchase time, rest before serving?

42. How long should the spiral screw on the corkscrew be?

43. Should the screw be hollow or solid?

44. What is a *sommelier*?

45. What type of tool do you use if the cork has broken in the neck of the bottle?

46. Why do you pierce the cork slightly off center in the process of removing it?

47. What is the most important reason for decanting?

48. What is the minimum amount of time, before decanting, that a bottle of sedimented wine should stand upright?

49. How do you maximize aeration in the decanting process while pouring?

50. Does a white wine need breathing time?

51. True/False: The younger the red, the more breathing time it needs.

52. Where are the famed White Rock Cellars?

53. If a wine has a black currant fragrance and taste, what wine might it be?

54. True/False: The size of the bottle plays an important part in the longevity of wine.

55. What wines should be served with oysters?

56. Name three wines that should be served with a pâté.

57. Name four types of fortified wines that do not have to be kept in a horizontal position.

58. Does it matter if the neck of the bottle is angled slightly up or down?

59. True/False: Any wines capped and not corked are ready to be opened when purchased.

60. What was the first vintage year Claret to appear in a Christie's catalog?

61. What percent of alcohol will result from one (1) percent of sugar?

62. Grape varieties used in the production of wine usually contain what percent sugar?

63. What is the meaning of "Auslese"?

64. What is an enologist?

65. What is *vin mousseux*?

66. What are Coteaux Champenois?

67. Name the bottle of wine auctioned for $31,000 in 1980, the most expensive bottle of wine up to that date.

68. The charity wine tasting held in 1981 in Memphis, at which the 1822 Château Lafite was opened, was a benefit for what charity?

69. What is the term used for the space between the cork and the top of the liquid?

70. What year did Christie's hold its first U.S. wine auction?

71. Where was Christie's first U.S wine auction held?

72. How many U.S. wine auctions are held by Christie's every year?

73. What year did Sotheby's hold its first American wine auction?

74. Who is the director of Sotheby's Wine Department who holds the title "Master of Wine"?

75. What month and year was the first Napa Valley Wine Auction held?

76. At the first Napa Valley Wine Auction, a noted wine merchant named Charles Mara purchased a case of wine for $24,000. This case was jointly bottled by what two famous vintners?

77. What is the name of the country club that hosts the Napa Valley Wine Auction?

78. What distinguished the labels on the case of Kenwood Vineyards 1975 Cabernet Sauvignon that sold for $480 at the Sonoma County Wine Auction?

79. What was pictured on the labels from Kenwood Vineyards 1975 Cabernet Sauvignon?

80. Who runs the KQED (San Francisco's PBS station) International Wine Auction?

81. One type of Champagne glass commonly used is the elongated tulip shape. Name the two other shapes frequently used.

82. In storing wineglasses, should they be stored upside down or upright, and why?

83. Name three famous wine auction houses.

84. Heublein held its first wine auction in America in what year?

85. What company is the second largest wine producer in the United States?

86. Name three of four basic elements to keep in mind in selecting your wineglasses.

87. What type of wine glass is traditionally used for table reds?

88. How much does the traditional tulip wine glass ideally hold?

89. Name two or three differences between the tulip wine glass and the Paris goblet.

90. What king ordered the wine makers to design a glass made for the Burgundy reds?

91. Name two out of three differences between a white wine glass and a red wine glass.

92. The standard glass for Sherry, Port and Madeira is called "the little cup." What is its Spanish name?

93. True/False: The sweeter the wine, the cooler its serving temperature.

94. What is the ideal serving temperature range of sweet white wines?

95. What is the ideal serving temperature range for a dry white wine?

96. What is the ideal serving temperature of a young red wine such as a Beaujolais?

97. What is the ideal serving temperature for the red wines of the Loire red Bordeaux or domestic Burgundy?

98. What is a *tastevin*?

99. What is a properly prepared ice bucket?

100. During pouring, how much should each glass hold?

101. In the Bordeaux region, what type of cheese is traditionally served with a Sauternes?

102. What do cheese, bread, and wine all have in common?

103. What is pH?

104. How is it measured?

105. What is the range of pH figures for wine?

106. What two vintners have claimed the name Stag's Leap and are now engaged in an effort to prevent a "Stag's Leap" appellation?

107. When did Robert Mondavi purchase his own vineyard?

108. What best-selling author is part owner of Creston-Manor Vineyards & Winery?

109. What are the five U.S. cities that the Beaujolais Nouveau is flown to on November 15th of each year?

110. What is a "corky" wine?

111. Who created the wine known in California as Fumé Blanc?

112. With what wine is the word "crusted" associated?

113. What is Commanderia?

114. What does the word *cru* mean?

115. What is a *Dame-Jeanne*?

116. In what book of the Bible is wine first mentioned?

117. How many ounces of wine in a magnum?

118. What is Ekri Bikaver?

119. What is the principal grape in Hungary's famous Tokay wine?

120. What is Bristol Milk?

121. What wine comes in the greatest variety of sized bottles?

122. What is the difference between a foudre, a quartant, a barrique and a demi-muid?

123. Heat is an enemy of wine, yet there is one wine that is baked as part of the process to develop it. What wine is it?

124. If a wine is said to be "foxy" in taste, from what basic grape family does the grape come?

125. Despite the bad press Eastern American grape varieties get, what California classic has its origin in New England?

126. What are lees?

127. How many different herbs, seeds, spices, etc., can be used in the making of Vermouth?

128. What is the generic name of Vermouth?

129. What are the four most popular fortified wines?

130. What is America's contribution to fortified wines?

131. Why did Noah dislike water?

132. Which state in the United States was famous for its wines before the Civil War (not New York)?

133. What was St. Paul's advice to his friend Timothy?

134. What is the difference between Chablis and Petit Chablis?

135. In what year did Larry Bender of Boston break the world's record for the price of a single (750 ml) bottle of wine?

136. What did he pay?

137. What was the wine, the producer and the vintage year?

138. What was the previous world record?

139. What was the event at which the wine was sold?

140. Who was the auctioneer?

141. What does "M.W." after a name mean?

142. In what city is the Zinfandel Club located?

143. There are 32 major and minor wine competitions in the United States. Name the top eight.

144. What are the five "noble" grapes from which most of the world's great wines are made?

145. Which two grapes would Italian winemakers add to that list?

146. What do Barolo, Spanna and Gattinara wines have in common?

147. What are shot berries?

148. What is a "sick" wine?

149. Château Lafite Rothschild once produced a second label wine. What was its name?

150. Where is the Christian Brothers Winery?

151. What does a wine taster mean if he says a wine tastes *goût de terroir*?

152. What was California's first recorded vintage year?

153. Who were the producers?

154. Where was their vineyard located?

155. What type of wine did they produce?

156. Who has the largest collection of carved wine barrels in North America?

157. When were the first wine grapes planted in Napa Valley?

158. Count Agoston Haraszthy's original vineyard was named what?

159. Where was it located?

160. What were the first three "appellations" of California?

161. The Pellier brothers (circa 1880's) were the founders of what famous winery?

162. There's been no "juicy" wine scandal in the United States for years. When was the first one and what were the circumstances?

163. Where was the *phylloxera* louse first identified?

164. *Vitis vinifera* is the classic European grape family that produces the world's great wines. What is the root stock that saved the *vinifera* vines from extinction by the *phylloxera*?

165. Do you remember the Italian Swiss Colony "little ole winemaker"? Who used to interview him?

166. Most people believe that Prohibition started in 1919, but in reality it has been with us for many years. Which state was the first to ban alcoholic beverages?

167. Prior to Prohibition, Americans consumed 0.53 gallons of wine per capita. How much wine did they consume *during* Prohibition?

168. What was the favorite grape of wine bootleggers?

169. When did Ernesto and Julio Gallo begin making wine?

170. Louis Pasteur is famous for his discovery of "pasteurization," the process by which milk is rendered germ-free. What was Pasteur actually working on when he discovered "pasteurization"?

171. How many times is wine mentioned in the Old Testament?

172. How many times is it mentioned in the New Testament?

173. Who is known as the Greek wine god?

174. Wine can be stored in many different containers, but when did the classic Bordeaux bottle first make its appearance?

175. What are the three basic acids found in grapes?

176. While California claims to be the scene of the first wineries in the United States, where was the first wine in America made?

177. How many states in the United States produce wine?

178. What wine is produced in Hawaii?

179. What was the first commercial vineyard in the United States?

180. Where Union Station now stands in Los Angeles was once the scene of California's first vineyards. Who owned it and what year was the vineyard planted?

181. How many vine growing regions are there in California?

182. How many climate regions are there in California?

183. What is the difference between Region I and Region V?

15

184. Latour is a famous name in California winemaking as well as in French. Name the man and the vineyard he founded in Napa Valley.

185. The owner of the Clos du Val vineyard is the son of a former Maître de Chai of Château Lafite Rothschild. What is the son's name?

186. Wine runs in the Portet family's blood. Name his brother's winery and where it is located.

187. A former candidate for president of the United States grows his own grapes and makes excellent wines. Who is he?

188. Two show business brothers also have their own prize-winning winery in Sonoma Valley. Name them.

189. In 1976, a surprise blind tasting of California vs. French wines was held in Paris. A Napa Valley winery fooled the French experts and was pronounced better than the premier *grand cru's* of Bordeaux. Which winery was it?

190. What is the owner's name?

191. Moët et Chandon make Champagne in France. They make sparkling wine in California. What is the name of their winery in California?

192. The man who directed *The Godfather* is a winemaker too. What is his name?

193. Who owned bonded winery license number one in New York State?

194. Which winery owns the biggest vineyard in Napa Valley?

195. Who is their winemaker and cellar-master?

196. Brother Timothy is famous for having a collection of the most important devices in the wine business. What are they?

197. What did Robert Louis Stevenson say about California wine?

198. The first woman winemaker in California was Doña Marcelina Felix Dominguez who proved that drinking wine can add years to your life. How old was she when she died?

199. As we have had wine since time immemorial, we have had wine critics. Who was the first wine critic in California?

200. Who is considered the "father" of the Sonoma Valley wine industry?

201. Zinfandel is a grape whose ancestry is still in doubt. What is one of the earliest known records of the grape?

202. What was the early (circa mid-1800's) name for the Zinfandel?

203. Colonel Agoston Haraszthy is often mentioned as the person who introduced the Zinfandel to California. He wasn't. Who was?

204. Zinfandel is grown in all five temperature regions of California. Which area produces the highest quality wine?

205. How many different styles of Zinfandel wine can be made?

206. Wine made from the Aleatico grape in California would be known as what wine in Italy?

207. Inglenook Winery is noted for many excellent wines, but one particular wine is a favorite of the owners. What is it?

208. The grape known as Shiraz in Australia is known as what in California?

209. Those elegant California Chardonnays have a "flinty" quality to them. What is this known as in French?

210. Making good wine means attention to details such as keeping the barrels of wine topped off so that they won't oxidize. What is a famous German saying regarding this practice?

211. Chardonnay wasn't always popular as a crop for California grape growers. Who was the pioneer Chardonnay producer?

212. The first Sauvignon Blanc grapes planted in California came from what famous French vineyard in Bordeaux?

213. How does the University of California at Davis describe the taste of the Sauvignon Blanc wine?

214. The Sauvignon Blanc combined with what other grape makes the classic Sauternes of France?

215. Chenin Blanc is a popular wine that goes under what other names?

216. What white wine grape's name would remind you of a fast food chain?

217. Who made the first sparkling wines in America?

218. What grape did he use?

219. Who was the first Californian to make sparkling wine?

220. In making sparkling wine, what is the difference between the transfer process and the *charmat* process?

221. What is Panache?

222. Name the single (as of this writing) wine producer who makes all his kosher wines from *vinifera* grapes.

223. Must the wine used in the Roman Catholic Mass be made exclusively of grapes?

224. What noted Victorian author published a book on American wine?

225. If a California wine label states that the wine in the bottle is Burgundy, what particular grape must be represented in the bottle?

226. If the label states an established viticultural area such as Sonoma, what percentage of the wine must have been made in that area?

227. A "fat" wine does not mean the wine is highly caloric. What does that term mean?

228. What is the legal upper limit of alcohol in dessert wines?

229. What does "estate bottled" mean on a California wine label?

230. Brother Timothy, F.S.C., the world-renowned corkscrew collector, notes that the first patented corkscrew was designed in what year and by whom?

231. Who was the inventor of the "waiter's corkscrew"?

232. Why is the "Ah-So" cork puller known as the "butler's friend"?

233. What is Hugh Johnson's opinion of the cork?

234. What rank does the United States hold in wine production?

235. What rank does the United States hold when it comes to wine consumption?

236. Who is number one in wine consumption?

237. What is the most widely planted varietal wine grape in California?

238. California produces 95% of the wine in the United States. Of that total, what percentage is produced by the top 10%?

239. How many bonded wineries are there in California?

240. How many bonded wineries in the other 49 states?

241. Which county in California has the most wineries?

242. Of course, Gallo is the largest winery in the United States. How does it rank worldwide?

243. What type of wine is favored by American wine drinkers?

244. What was the name of the popular sparkling wine of the '60s and '70s?

245. What was the origin of the name "Cold Duck"?

246. What percentage of the United States adult population consumes wine every day or almost every day?

247. Which class consumes the most wine, the professional or the blue-collar worker?

248. Which sections of the United States consume the most wine?

249. What is the difference between French wine drinkers and American wine drinkers?

250. One of Napa Valley's magnificent Victorian mansions is seen regularly on TV. Name the show and name the man who built the home in 1880.

251. When was the first federal tax imposed on wine?

252. When was the first federal tax imposed on domestic wine?

253. When California finally became the biggest wine producing state in the nation, what state did it surpass?

254. What are the three senses used in judging the quality of a wine?

255. When once asked whether he had ever confused Bordeaux and Burgundy, the great English winetaster Harry Waugh said what?

256. Wine grapes grow best in the temperate zone. What are the northern and southern extremes of latitude in which grapes may be grown to maturity?

257. Halley's Comet might appear this year. What was the rating of the wine produced when it last appeared in 1910?

258. Is every year a "vintage" year in the Champagne region?

259. Madeira is a fine wine, yet if a wine is "maderized," it's bad. What causes maderization?

260. Tokay, the great wine from Hungary

comes from a small district about 30 miles from the Russian border. Tokay sounds romantic, but the river that flows through the district has the unromantic name of what?

261. Tokay Essence is probably the oldest living wine in existence, exceeding even Madeira. To what is this long life attributed?

262. Tokay Aszu is a sweet wine. What is the term used to indicate the degree of sweetness in a Tokay?

263. Many cities in the United States are named "Quincy." There is a town in France also named Quincy (Can-see). What kind of wine is produced in Quincy, France?

264. An odd name for a wine is Rainwater. What type of wine is it?

265. Is Saki wine?

266. What is rosé wine?

267. When was cork first used as a stopper in a wine bottle?

268. What is the chemical (natural) that causes wine made from Labrusca grapes to taste "foxy"?

269. What is *tête de cuvée*?

270. What is Retsina?

271. What is Persian Poison?

272. What is the significance of the Jewish toast *L'Chayim*?

273. Some tasters describe a wine as being "dumb." What do they mean by that term?

274. What causes a wine to be astringent?

275. An American sparkling wine took prizes in European competitions in 1873, 1889 (in Paris), 1897 and 1900. Name the winery and where it is located.

276. Under what name can you find that sparkling wine today?

277. A newspaper editor was the first person to import French hybrid grape vines into the United States. Name the paper he worked for and his name.

278. What was the name of the first man who planted grape vines in the Finger Lakes region of New York State?

279. Dr. Konstantin Frank was not the first grape farmer to plant *vinifera* grapes in the East. Who preceded him in New York State?

280. M. Fournier and Dr. Frank together sought *vinifera* roots that could withstand the severe cold of the Northeast. Where did they find such roots?

281. During Prohibition, "grape bricks" were sold which, when water was add-

ed to them, would make grape juice. With each "brick" came a yeast pill and a warning. What did the warning advise?

282. Benjamin Franklin, like his contemporary Thomas Jefferson, loved wine. What is his most famous quote regarding wine?

283. Napa Valley is one of the great California tourist attractions. Before the vineyards, what Indian tribe inhabited the area?

284. What name did they give the valley?

285. The Napa Valley has seen three nations vie for its possession. Name them.

286. The grape planting Franciscan fathers established their 21st and last mission in Sonoma. In what section was this mission established?

287. Who was the first American to settle in Napa Valley?

288. The wines the Franciscan fathers made were always considered "Mexican wine (from the Mission grape)." Who was the first grape farmer who made wine from *vinifera* grapes?

289. Who owns the Krug Winery today?

290. Mr. Krug made 8,250 gallons of wine in 1860. Guess, to within 100,000 gallons, how much he made the year he died in 1890?

291. When the British signed the Treaty of Methuen in 1703, what wine "suddenly" became popular in England?

292. In 1973, Jerry Luper, then winemaker at Freemark Abbey, Napa Valley, made a wine that he called "Edelweine." From what grapes did he make this wine?

293. It was acclaimed by all as comparable to what type of German wine?

294. There are two Martha's Vineyards in the United States. Which one has bonded winery license number one for its state?

295. Where is the other Martha's Vineyard?

296. What was the first name of the Cabernet Sauvignon grape?

297. In the University of California at Davis wine evaluation scale, what one factor counts the most?

298. The Hedonic wine evaluation scale is based on 9 points. What is the highest rated classification?

299. The word "symposium" has a weighty connotation, but in ancient days, what did it mean?

300. Who presided over these happy affairs?

301. The Greeks were much enamoured of wine. Besides Bacchus, they gave us the Hippocras. What was it?

302. Who invented the barrel?

303. What is the oldest California Cabernet Sauvignon now available to the public?

304. Of the vast quantity of wine produced in France, how much of the annual 1.7 billion gallons is better than ordinary?

305. America and Russia share a practice that the French find despicable. Each nation uses French wine names on their wine labels. What do the Russians call Champagne?

306. Dr. Frank was one of the first, along with Charles Fournier, to propagate *vinifera* vines, but many others before him tried. Who were some of the more famous ones?

307. What brand of wine sponsored the first singing commercial for its product?

308. What French wines did the same thing many years before?

309. Although South Carolina is more famous for corn whiskey than wine, it is famous as the birthplace of what three American wine grapes?

310. Who wrote *Ode to Catawba Wine*?

311. Before Coca-Cola became America's most famous soft drink, what was the most popular drink in America?

312. There are only a few Cepages Nobles grapes, those that produce the classic great wines, but how many different types of grapes are commercially raised for wine?

313. In the Chablis district of Burgundy, what is the local nickname for Chardonnay?

314. What is the Pinot Blanc known as in Germany?

315. The Riesling grape not only makes a fine wine, but is the proud parent of how many other superior grape varieties?

316. Is Grey Riesling a true Riesling grape?

317. Gewürztraminer is a noble grape and one of those jaw-breaking German names. Where did this wonderful grape come from?

318. What grape shares its name with a breed of horse?

319. Of all the wineries in California, which can continuously trace its ancestry back to the beginning days?

320. Etienne Theé had a partner whose name appears on Almaden's premium brand. Who was he?

321. There was yet another winemaking Frenchman who became related to Charles Lefranc. Who was he?

322. Who was the man who made Beaulieu's Private Reserve Cabernet the great wine that it has been since the 1930's?

323. What is the varietal wine whose given name will remind you of a seasick middle-European?

324. Forty-eight varieties of grapes are permitted to be used in the making of Port wine. How many are red grapes and how many are white?

325. Sledgehammers used to be used to drill holes to plant vines on the incredibly steep banks of the Douro River. What is used now?

326. What wine did Carmen offer Don José to tempt him to desert the army?

327. French oak is often used to mature wines. With what European wine is American oak used?

328. Aging sherry in American oak doesn't end the barrel's usefulness. How else is it used?

329. Before the grapes that make sherry are crushed, they are sprinkled with gypsum. Who first recommended that this be done (about 2 pounds of gypsum to 1,500 pounds of grapes)?

330. Why is this done?

331. Dry Sack is a name for a certain brand

of sherry today. What is the origin of the word "sack" in reference to sherry?

332. Marsala, the fine fortified wine from Sicily, was invented by whom?

333. What were the names of the two scouts who brought Moses a bunch of grapes from Palestine?

334. "A rose by any other name," said Shakespeare, "would smell as sweet." Does a name change for a grape alter its ability to make good wine?

335. To what does the term "free run" refer?

336. To what does the term *vin de presse* refer?

337. Despite all the trouble it has seen, what country in the Middle East continues to produce wine?

338. In the winemaking business, what is a "thief"?

339. To what does the term *espalier* refer?

340. What is *galgenwein*?

341. A "gourmet" in America is a person who appreciates fine food. What does the term mean in Alsace?

342. What is a *halbstück*?

343. What is the difference between Rioja and La Rioja?

344. What wine did Cleopatra serve Caesar?

345. Where does Mavrodaphne wine come from?

346. Is "mascara" merely a form of eye make-up?

347. What is *muselage*?

348. An octave is a musical term also used in the winemaking trade. What does it mean in winemaking?

349. What do *botrytis cinerea, pourriture noble* and *edelfaule* have in common?

350. What is a *chapeau*?

351. At a wine tasting party, what color should the table cloth be?

352. Bread and cheese are a "must" at a wine tasting. What is the trade axiom about wine, bread and cheese?

353. If a wine is said to be "acetic," what can you expect in the taste?

354. If a person describes a wine as "well-balanced," what is meant?

USA

1. Who were the first to plant vineyards in California?

2. What were the first *vinifera* grapes grown in the eastern United States?

3. Who is the "Father of California Viticulture"?

4. What is grape louse?

5. When did grape louse nearly obliterate the American wine industry?

6. How did the wine industry recover from the outbreak of *phylloxera*?

7. What is the first winery established in "America's Home Town"?

8. Who said, "The smack of California earth shall linger on the palate of your grandson"?

9. Who was the first to successfully market the Zinfandel?

10. What is the meaning of *Napa* as in Napa Valley?

11. What is the most significant wine of Napa Valley?

12. What is the basic difference between the French Bordeaux and the Cabernet Sauvignon?

13. What are the six major white wine grapes of California?

14. What is the most largely produced grape in California?

15. What is the most widely produced wine in Washington?

16. What is the only white Zinfandel to receive three gold medals in one year?

17. What is the second largest wine-making state after California?

18. What types of wines are particularly notable from this area?

19. What grapes are commonly used in the production of fortified wines from New York?

20. What is the most famous wine-growing area of New York?

21. What are two other significant areas in New York?

22. What great winery, located near Hammondsport in the Finger Lakes region,

is noted for both premium and Champagne wines?

23. Who acquired this company (previous answer) in 1962?

24. Who currently owns Taylor Wine Company?

25. What is Taylor Wine especially noted for?

26. What is said to be the smallest "bonded winery" in America?

27. What is the oldest exclusively "estate" winery in New York?

28. What is the only winery in the east to be owned and operated entirely by women?

29. Who is the owner of Bully Hill Vineyards?

30. Who is the founder of the Vinifera Wine Cellars?

31. What was he doing in the 1950s?

32. What are hybrid wines?

33. What are some of the hybrids used in New York?

34. What indigenous grapes are used in New York?

35. Name three *vinifera* grapes which are successfully grown currently in New York.

36. What is de Chaunac?

37. What are the best known wines of the Finger Lakes region?

38. Who is Seyve-Villard?

39. What is the Niagra?

40. What is the French hybrid produced from the Pinot Noir and the Gamay?

41. What winery produces the Charles Fournier Champagne?

42. What is the largest grape growing district in the east?

43. What is the second most widely grown American wine grape?

44. What is Canada's largest winery?

45. Who is Philip Wagner?

46. What grape was once known as Seibel 5279?

47. What is the first winery in Idaho?

48. What is the largest vineyard in Washington?

49. What country in the Western Hemisphere produces the largest amount of wine?

50. What does "produced and bottled by" mean?

51. True/False: Alcoholic content is required on the label.

52. When was Prohibition signed into law?

53. What did the vineyards of America do to survive Prohibition?

54. When was it repealed?

55. When were the first "blind tastings" conducted in America?

56. What was the original purpose of blind tastings?

57. What wine was first advertised in New York in 1945 and soon became the most widely known wine in North America?

58. What is the predominant kosher wine grape?

59. Who first introduced this grape?

60. All kosher wines must bear what on the label?

61. Who is credited with the emergence and ultimate popularity of kosher wines in America?

62. What kosher food company did Leo Star contract with to use its name?

63. What was the largest competitor of Manischewitz?

64. What does *Mogen David* mean?

65. Who founded the first commercial vineyard in California?

66. Who is given credit for introducing the Catawba grape?

67. Who was the first to cultivate grapes in the Finger Lakes district of New York?

68. When was the Wine Institute incorporated?

69. When did federal wine label and quality standards become effective?

70. What institution introduced the Emerald Riesling in 1946?

71. When was the American Society of Enologists organized?

72. What is *must*?

73. In what way does a California Sauterne differ from a French Sauternes?

74. Who was Fred McCrea?

75. Who owns Sterling Vineyards?

76. Where is Beringer located?

77. What is the Charbono?

78. What two profiles appear on the label of Opus One?

79. What wine is Stag's Leap most noted for?

80. What is unique about the approach to Sterling Vineyards?

81. What are the four premium wines of Sterling wineyards?

82. Who founded Stonegate Winery?

83. What is the wine producing area of Santa Clara County called?

84. When a California wine label includes a vintage date, what percentage of the grapes used for the wine must have been harvested during that year?

85. When a California wine label names a winery as the producer and bottler, what percentage of the wine must be fermented by the named winery?

86. When a California wine label bears the grape variety and was produced prior to January 1983, what percentage of the wine must be derived from that grape? What percentage for wines produced *after* January 1983?

87. When the label includes a recognized viticultural area, (i.e. Napa, Sonoma, Russian River, etc.), what is the minimum percentage of grapes that must come from that area?

88. What famous war correspondent purchased Buena Vista Winery at auction shortly after World War II?

89. What famous vineyard, founded by German brothers, uses a structure

called the "Rhine House" as a tasting room and a starting point for wine tours?

91. What does "prepared or cellared and bottled by" mean?

92. What two vineyards in the Napa Valley produce Charbono?

93. What California winery founder and winemaker is retired from the San Francisco Fire Department?

94. Who named Fumé Blanc?

95. What is the grape usually blended with Sauvignon Blanc to make Fumé Blanc?

96. According to Ripley, what winery had a "cellar in the clouds"?

97. What winery founder featured his grandson on a wine label?

FRANCE

1. What are *fillettes*?

2. When is *chaptalisation* (adding sugar before fermentation) authorized for château wines?

3. What was the purpose of having estate-bottled wines?

4. Can château wines ever be blended with wines from outside the limits of the château?

5. What is the name of the insect that nearly destroyed the great vineyards of Bordeaux in the 1860's?

6. What country had vineyards which were immune to root louse?

7. How was this problem finally solved?

8. What was the first Bordeaux red put down for aging?

9. What is the official classification in Pomerol?

10. What is the predominant grape used in Pomerol wines?

11. What are Blanc de Blancs?

12. In France, what is a commune?

13. How many growths of the 1855 classification (Médoc) are there?

14. What is the only "First Great Growth" of Sauternes?

15. What is the first rank of St. Emilion classed growths (1954 classification)?

16. What is the second rank of St. Emilion classed growths?

17. What is the only wine growing region of France to be classed in 1955 outside of Médoc?

18. What is the largest commune in Sauternes?

19. What is the French term for the Bordeaux first growth wines of the 1855 Médoc classification?

20. What famous American artist painted the image that appears on the upper half of the 1975 Château Mouton-Rothschild label?

21. What event in 1977 led to the design of the 1977 Château Mouton-Rothschild label?

22. Which current Médoc first growth is the only one to be added since the original classification of 1855?

23. Which of the current first growths of the 1855 Bordeaux classification is not in Médoc?

24. What are the principal communes of Médoc?

25. From what district comes the great wine Petrus?

26. Why is it difficult, if not impossible, to ascertain the quality of Château d'Yquem until years after the grapes are harvested?

27. What is the term for the "shipper" of wine?

28. What famous artist painted the image on the upper half of the Châteaux Mouton Rothschild 1979 label?

29. What is the French term for vintage?

30. How many districts are there in Bordeaux?

31. Which are the five most famous districts in Bordeaux?

32. Which of these districts are renowned for their reds?

33. What type of wine gives fame to Sauternes?

34. Médoc is divided into two areas: what are they?

35. The best wines of Médoc come from which of these two areas?

36. Haut-Médoc is divided into 28 municipalities, which are called what?

37. What is the largest Bordeaux wine district?

38. What is the name of the wide estuary connecting the Atlantic Ocean and the main wine growing regions of Bordeaux?

39. What two rivers form the northern and southern borders of Entre-Deux- Mers?

40. What is the predominant red wine grape used in Bordeaux?

41. What other red wine grapes are used in Bordeaux?

42. What is the white grape used to make Sauternes sweet wines?

43. What great poet established Château Ausone?

44. What grapes are used to produce white Bordeaux wines?

45. What first growths come from Pauillac?

46. What first growths come from Margaux?

47. How do the British refer to red Bordeaux wine?

48. What event in the 12th century had the effect of bringing the wines of

Bordeaux to the awareness of the British?

49. What is the meaning of *chai*?

50. Who is the *maître de chai*?

51. What is an *égrappoir*?

52. What is *marc*?

53. What two second growths come from Pauillac?

54. Besides the first growths of Pauillac, what are two of the most celebrated estates there?

55. Who owns Château Haut-Brion?

56. What is the most celebrated vineyard in St. Emilion?

57. In order for a *vin mousseaux* to have an *appellation controllé* (A.C.), what is the first requirement?

58. What are the best known wines from the Loire?

59. What is the *Charmat* method?

60. Where is Provence?

61. Who were the first to cultivate vineyards in Provence?

62. What is the largest single appellation in Provence?

63. What are the four other appellations of Provence?

64. What great wine exporting city is situated on the western corner of Provence?

65. What is the historical significance of the village of LaGaude?

66. What is the most significant type of wine made in Provence?

67. What is the most celebrated wine of Côtes du Rhône?

68. What is the oldest of French sparkling wines?

69. What is the famous sweet white wine from Southwest France used for the christening of King Henry IV?

70. When were the French *appellation controllée* laws passed?

71. What do the *appellation controllée* laws guarantee?

72. What are *vins de café*?

73. What wine has the legal minimum alcohol strength of any French wine?

74. What French writer was the first to write a book about the wines aging in his basement?

75. What is the French name given to Burgundy?

76. Name the northernmost wine growing regions of Burgundy.

77. What are the three southern important wine growing regions of Burgundy?

78. Côte d'Or is divided into what two parts?

79. Burgundy's major white wines are made from what grape?

80. The red wines of Mâconnais are made from what grape?

81. The red wines of Côte d'Or are made from what grape?

82. The red wines of the Chalonnais are made from what grape?

83. The famous Beaujolais reds are made from what grape?

84. What grape is used in making the wine with the appellation of Bourgogne Aligoté?

85. What grapes are used in making the blend which carries the appellation of Bourgogne Passe Tout-Grains?

86. Up until the French Revolution, who owned the majority of the best vineyards in Burgundy?

87. What happened after the Revolution?

88. What is the meaning of *Mis en Bouteille à la Propriété*?

89. What is another phrase which appears on the Burgundy wine label meaning the same thing?

90. In Côte d'Or the wines carry two classifications; what are they?

91. Give an example of each.

92. Geographically, what is the significance of Burgundy?

93. What is the meaning of the Burgundian word *climat*?

94. Why do wine growing properties, especially in this area, have the tendency to get smaller as time passes?

95. Why is it difficult to predict consistency in the wines of Burgundy?

96. Generally, how long are the Burgundy reds aged before bottling?

97. What is the highest, most distinguished appellation of Burgundian wines?

98. What type of wine is this?

99. What is the second appellation?

100. What type of wine is this?

101. Which of these classifications only identify the name of the vineyard?

102. What is the first red wine village of the Côtes de Nuits?

103. What famous village is the location of eight Grand Cru vineyards of Côtes de Nuits?

104. How can these great wines be identified?

105. Why is red Burgundy less long-lived than red Bordeaux?

106. How many Grand Cru's come from Morey-Saint-Denis?

107. What is the largest vineyard in Burgundy?

108. Who owns the vineyard?

109. What is the house of the famed Romanée-Conti?

110. How many Grand Cru's are there in Burgundy?

111. What is the distinguishing factor of the labels of Grand Cru and Premier Cru?

112. What is the largest vineyard in Côte de Nuits?

113. What is the only Grand Cru red in Côte de Beaune?

114. What is referred to as the "wine center" of Burgundy?

115. How would you characterize most of the red wines of Beaujolais?

116. What are the four grades of Beaujolais?

117. What is the difference between Beaujolais and Beaujolias Supérior?

118. Where does Beaujolais-Villages come from?

119. Where does Cru Beaujolais come from?

120. On what date is Beaujolais-Nouveaux released?

121. What is the minimum alcohol content of Beaujolais grade wine?

122. What is Beaunois?

123. What river runs through Chablis?

124. How many appellations are there in Chablis?

125. What is the top appellation for Chablis?

126. What is the second ranked appellation?

127. Besides the appellation, what other differences are there between Grand Cru and Premier Cru?

128. How many Grand Crus are there?

129. From where in Burgundy does Pouilly-Fuissé come?

130. Name three white wine names of Côte de Beaune?

131. The third Burgundian appellation is what?

132. What type of wines are the third appellations?

133. What are the final two appellations?

134. Where is Alsace and what are the predominant geographical features of the area?

135. What unique feature of the Alsace wine label sets it apart from nearly all other French wines labels?

136. What historical reasons account for the similarities of Alsace and German wines?

137. What color wine bottles are used for the wines of Alsace?

138. What is the term used to describe the shape of the bottle used for the Alsatian wines?

139. The best wines of Alsace carry what qualifications on the label?

140. What is the significance of Cuveé Spéciale or Reserve when seen on Alsatian wine labels?

141. When the vineyard appears on the Alsatian wine label, what does it mean?

142. What is Edelzwicker?

143. When Edelzwicker appears on the label, what grape(s) are used?

144. The wines of Alsace use grapes which are called *noble* and lesser varieties. What are the three most common "lesser" grapes?

145. When the terms Grand Cru, Grand Réserve, or Reśerve Exceptionnelle appear on the label, what can be said of the alcohol content?

146. What is Zwicker?

147. What is *vin gris*?

148. What grape is most frequently used in making *vin gris*?

149. Of the noble grape varieties used in Alsatian wines, which is the most celebrated?

150. How would you characterize the taste of this wine?

151. What is the second most planted grape in Alsace?

152. What is Tokay d'Alsace?

153. What is the other name for Tokay D'Alsace?

154. Is there any connection with the Tokay of Hungary?

155. What are some of the differences between Alsatian and German wines using the same grape varieties?

156. What is the meaning of *cepage*?

157. What is the meaning of *vendage tardive*?

158. What is a *brasserie*?

159. What is the meaning of *cuvée particuliére*?

160. What is the meaning of *Vin d'Alsace*?

161. What is the basic difference in taste between French Alsace Riesling and German Reisling?

162. What is the only blended wine of Alsace?

163. What two French cities make the northern and southern extremities of the Côtes du Rhône?

164. What is Avignon historically famous for?

165. Which pope was the first to make his residence in Avignon?

166. What is the original meaning of the *Châteauneuf-du-Pape*?

167. What is the predominant wine of the Rhône?

168. In what region of the Rhône is this wine (previous answer) produced?

169. What is the most famous wine of the Rhône?

170. What is the principal grape of this wine?

171. What is the significance of the Syrah grape variety?

172. What great American historical figure came to the Rhône and made the following statement about Rhône wine: "Keeps well, bears transportation and cannot be drunk under four years"?

173. What particular wine was he referring to?

174. What are the two appellations of the Rhône?

175. What is Hermitage famous for?

176. How would you describe the taste of wines from Côtes du Rhône?

177. What geographic conditions of the area lend itself to these qualities?

178. What is the most widely used black grape in southern Côtes du Rhône?

179. What is the Viognier?

180. Where does it come from?

181. How many communes carry the appellation "Côtes du Rhône Villages"?

182. What is the "roasted hillside"?

183. What appellations do the best Rhône wines carry?

184. What are Cornas wines?

185. What is Clairette de Die?

186. What is Tavel famous for?

187. How is the pink color of these wines achieved?

188. What grape is used for the rosés of Tavel?

189. What other areas near Tavel also produce pink wines?

190. What is Rasteau?

191. What other region besides the Rhône valley produced Châteauneuf-du-Pape?

192. What shaped bottle is used for Châteauneuf-du-Pape?

193. Name three or more of the celebrated Châteauneuf-du-Pape producers?

194. What wines, according to Professor Saintsburg, are the "manliest" on earth?

195. What wine producing village lies to the north of Hermitage?

196. Pouilly-sur-Loire is known as the home of what wine?

197. How would you characterize the taste of this wine?

198. What is the predominant grape used in the eastern Loire?

199. From what grape is the wine Pouilly-sur-Loire produced?

200. Directly across the river from Pouilly-sur-Loire is what celebrated wine producing area?

201. What are the differences between Pouilly-Fuissé and the Pouilly-Fumé?

202. What is the westernmost city on the Loire River?

203. What is the most predominant wine of the western Loire?

204. What wine from Loire do the British refer to as "Golden Guinea"?

205. What grape is used in making Muscadet?

206. What are the three appellations of Muscadet?

207. What is the alcohol limit of Muscadet?

208. What is the area to the east of Muscadet known for its rosés?

209. What is the favorite grape for these rosés?

210. Where is Touraine?

211. What three villages are allowed to add their names to the Touraine appellation?

212. What are the most widely used grapes from Touraine?

213. What is the most famous wine of Touraine?

214. In what varieties does this wine come?

215. What grape is used for this wine (previous answer)?

216. What is Sparkling Vouvray called?

217. What are the aging characteristics of the various Vouvray wines?

218. What are the most celebrated red wines of Loire?

219. What is the area immediately downstream (westward) of Vouvray?

220. What are the most widely produced wines in this area?

221. What is the largest estate in Pouilly?

222. The Irish, as well as the English, have had a great influence in the wine business. An Irishman was the mayor of Bordeaux and also gave a couple of châteaux part of their name. What was the name?

223. However, the Irish didn't stop there. Another man from County Galway got into the act. His name?

224. All right, are there anymore Irishmen hiding in the wine barrel?

225. Officially speaking, what is the date recognized by most as the day to crack the first bottle of Nouveau Beaujolais in Paris or any other city?

226. Who is the patron saint of French winemakers?

227. Grapes change names as they go from one country to another. The Trebbiano in Italy becomes what grape in France?

228. At which part of a meal would you serve Beaume de Venise wine?

229. In addition to their fame as two of the fine wines of the world, two Burgundian wine firms share what other distinction?

230. The Franco-Prussian war was costly to France, but what event that occurred at just about the same time (1870) cost the French even more?

231. Clos Vougeot is one of the great Burgundian vineyards. It has 128 acres and how many owners?

232. Clos Vougeot was founded by what order of monks?

233. Clos Vougeot is called the what of Burgundy?

234. What king divided the regions of Burgundy as they are today?

235. What is the last wine producing commune of the Côte d'Or?

236. Two of the most popular sayings about wine in Burgundy are what?

237. What is the French term or word for the bottle label?

238. From what region of France do Gigondas wines come from?

239. In France, "pot" is a wine bottle. What is its capacity?

240. In what year did Château Mouton-Rothschild attain its present classification of Crus Hors Classe (Premier Cru)?

241. What is a Bordeaux mixture?

CHAMPAGNE

1. What event in the 17th century changed Champagne's wines from essentially still wines to sparkling wines?

2. What is the white grape used in making Champagne?

3. Name the two black grapes.

4. What is the term used for Champagne made from only white grapes?

5. How does Champagne retain a "white" color when black grapes are used?

6. What varieties of Champagne wines are blended?

7. What is vintage Champagne?

8. What is a blend of wines from several years called?

9. In the process of production of Champagne, how many stages of fermentation are there?

10. What is *liqueur de tirage*?

11. How is Champagne made to "sparkle"?

12. What is the process of *remuage*?

13. How is the sediment removed?

14. By law, what three features must the Champagne cork have?

15. What is *brut*?

16. What is *extra sec*?

17. What is *sec*?

18. What is *demi-sec* or *doux*?

19. When would *brut* be served?

20. When is *demi-sec* served?

21. Why should Champagne be served in a tulip-shaped glass?

22. What is Blanc de Noir?

23. What does it mean if the Champagne label does not have a year printed on it?

24. What does *crémant* refer to?

25. What is pink Champagne?

26. What is the French term used to identify the Champagne method of making sparkling wine?

27. What great battle of World War I nearly destroyed Champagne?

28. What is the capital of Champagne?

29. What is *dosage*?

30. How are the wines of Champagne classified?

31. What are *pupitres*?

32. What is the meaning of *sur pointe*?

33. Who is the largest "shipper" of Champagne?

34. What is *tête du cuvée*?

35. What was the first *tête du cuvée*?

36. Bollinger is a noted Champagne house. It produces a Champagne that is labeled, in part, "R.D." What does the "R.D." mean?

37. How long does Bollinger permit the Champagne to remain "on the lees" or gather its sediment in the neck of the bottle?

38. Champagne is traditionally a white, bubbly wine. Was it always that way?

GERMANY

1. What section of Germany produces the most wine?

2. Nearly all of the vineyards of Germany lie along the shores of what four rivers?

3. Why is nearly 90% of the wine produced in Germany white wine?

4. What is a *gebiet*?

5. How many wine growing regions are there in Germany?

6. How many of these regions produce Rhine wines?

7. What region is most celebrated for its Rhine wines?

8. How many regions are there in Mosel?

9. Name them (it).

10. What is the meaning of *Spitzenweine*?

11. German laws currently divide wines into how many categories?

12. German table wines must have what alcohol content to be labeled Deutscher Tafelwein?

13. What is the significance of the control number on Qb.A wine labels?

14. What must appear on the label of Qb.A wines?

15. What is the German term which is the equivalent of "estate bottled"?

16. What is the most restrictive feature of QmP wines?

17. What is the minimum alcohol content of QmP wines?

18. What is the significance of this law?

19. What is *gallization*?

20. What are the restrictions on *gallization*?

21. How are QmP wines further graded?

22. What is the lowest category, and what does it mean?

23. When are grapes harvested for Kabinett wines?

24. What is the second category and what does it mean?

25. When are the grapes picked for wines with (previous answer) on the label?

26. Why (previous answer)?

27. What is the third category and what does it mean?

28. What is the fourth (next to highest) category?

29. What is the highest category of QmP wine?

30. In what category of Prädikat would you expect to find *botrytis cinerea*?

31. What are Eiswein wines?

32. What categories of wines will include Eiswein?

33. What information must be on the QmP label?

34. The German labels contain three other "place" categories other than region and vineyard — what are they?

35. What is a *grosslage*?

36. German wine laws were first passed in what year?

37. What is the word seen on German wine labels indicating "sweet"?

38. What does *trocken* mean?

39. What does *Weisswein* mean?

40. What does *"Sekt, Qualitats - schaum-wein"* mean?

41. What is the French equivalent of Deutscher Landwein?

42. What is Germany's most southerly district?

43. What two ways are German wines sold?

44. German wine bottles with brown glass contain wine from what region?

45. German wine bottles with green glass contain wine from what region?

46. What wines use the flagon-shaped bottle?

47. Three grape varieties account for 80% of all German wines — what are they?

48. How was the Müller-Thurgau first made?

49. Where is the Müller-Thurgau most successfully produced?

50. Under German wine law, when may a German wine label include the grape variety?

51. German wine labels carry geographical place names in what order?

52. Generally, what effect does sweetness have on the price of German wine?

53. The term "Liebfraumilch" may be applied to any wine from where?

54. Shakespeare referred to Rhine wines in what way?

55. More recently, the British refer to Rhine wines as what?

56. What is Konsumwein?

57. What is the closest equivalent to Liebfraumilch from the Moselle?

58. What is *süss-reserve*?

59. What is a Boxbeutel?

60. Where is the largest "co-operative" in Germany?

61. What is the most celebrated single estate of the Saar?

62. What is the "Great Ring of Trier"?

63. What is Trier known for?

64. How can the wines of the Ruwer be distinguished from the rest of those of Moselle?

65. What is a *weinkellerei*?

66. What does *Eigene Abfullung* mean?

67. What does *Aus eigenem Lesegut* mean?

68. What is Deutcher Sekt?

69. What is Perlwein?

70. What is Roseewein?

71. What is Rotwein?

72. In general terms, what can be said of the alcohol content of German wines?

73. What grapes produce German red wines?

74. What is the only district of Germany that specializes in red wine?

75. Karl Marx went to school in what famous city in the Saar?

76. What is the "wine capital" of Nahe?

77. What event had the effect of substantially reducing the number of vineyards in Germany?

78. What is the largest city (and producer of wine) in Baden-Württemberg?

79. What is the most famous vineyard of Nahe?

80. What is the most celebrated vineyard of the Mosel?

81. Under the new law, Bernkastel has two Grosslage names; what are they?

82. What is the largest commune in the Mosel?

83. What is the largest grape growing area in Germany?

84. Nearly all of the wine produced in this vineyard (previous answer) is what type?

85. What is the oldest wine growing region in Germany?

86. What phenomenon has the effect of compromising the harsh weather of the northerly latitudes of the German wine industry?

87. What are the three cross-bred varieties of the Riesling grape?

88. What is the meaning of "Prädikat?"

89. What is the principal grape of Rheinhessen?

90. What is the most advertised German wine in the world?

91. What type of wine is it (previous question)?

92. What city lies at the juncture of the Saar, Ruwer and the river Mosel?

93. Who were the first to make wine in this area?

94. What are the three districts of Rheinpfalz?

95. What is Nierstein noted for?

96. The wines of Schloss Vollrads come from what region?

97. What is the geographical significance of Schloss Johannisberg?

98. At what equivalent latitude in North America is Schloss Johannisberg?

99. German wine is divided into how many title categories?

100. Of the total amount of wine made in Germany, what percentage is red wine?

101. What is the dominant vine in Mittelheim?

102. What is the most important season of the year in German viticulture?

103. What would be the optimum weather characteristics for this season?

104. What is the meaning of *Lese*?

105. What is the Deutche Weinsiegel?

106. Who awards the gold, silver and bronze medals which appear on the bottle?

107. What is the Kelterfest?

108. What is *neie*?

109. What is Badisch Rotgold and how is it produced?

110. What is Strata Montana?

111. Where is Rheinland-Pfalz?

112. From what region come the "Wines of Steel"?

113. What is a *bestimmteh Anbaugebiete*?

114. What is the largest producer in the major German wine areas?

115. What is the smallest?

116. What is Prüfungsnummer?

117. What is Bacchus?

118. What is a *gemeinde*?

119. What does *halbtrocken* mean?

120. Where is the vineyard Jesuitengarten?

121. What is the most celebrated vineyard in Johannisberg?

122. What is a *keller*?

123. Who is the patron saint of wine in Germany?

ITALY

1. What is the most popular sparkling wine of Italy?

2. What two beverages are made from the local wine of Asti?

3. What do the firms Martini and Cinzano have in common?

4. What is the "Capital City" of Vermouth?

5. What are the two varieties of Italian Vermouth?

6. True/False: Italian wine labels usually identify the vineyards on the label.

7. Under the new laws, Italian wines are divided into how many "qualities"?

8. What is the lowest quality rating?

9. The label of this quality will identify _____ as the location of production.

10. What is the second or middle quality rating?

11. The highest quality Italian wines carry what rating?

12. How must a premium wine be packaged for shipping?

13. What is the most celebrated white wine from the Piemonte region of Italy?

14. What is the name of the large northeast region near the French border which some say yields Italy's best red wines?

15. Name the three best-known wines which come from Genoa and the coast of Liguria.

16. What is Liguria's most famous wine?

17. What is the name of the province which nearly divides Italy in half south of Milan and north of Florence?

18. What is the name of the grape named after the river which joins the Po at Plaienza?

19. What is the white wine of the village of Reggio?

20. What is the name of the fizzy red wine which, in addition to motor-cars, made the town of Modena famous?

21. What is the town of Bologna's white wine called?

22. From what region do we get Chianti?

23. From what two grapes is Brolio Bianco made?

24. True/False: The island of Elba, between Tuscany and Corsica, produces only red wine.

25. From which province do we get Orvieto?

26. What is the "Wine of Rome"?

27. Name the three villages which make a wine called Frascati.

28. Is Falernum, an ancient Roman wine, white or red?

29. True/False: Orvieto can be both red *and* white.

30. What unusually-named wine is produced in Montefiascone?

31. Who created this wine (previous answer)?

32. How many varieties of Italian wines are officially recognized as controlled denominations?

33. What is the name of the red seal inscribed with the letters "INE" necessary for all exported Italian

wines (coming into the U.S.A for con-sumption)?

34. What is Italy's smallest region, which produces only two D.O.C. wines?

35. Name the only two D.O.C. wines from the region named above.

36. What is the famous red wine from the Lombardy region made from dried grapes?

37. Name the three wines which make up the "Great Trio" of Veronese wines.

38. What region is known for producing "The Great Trio"?

39. Name the three colors in which the Pinot Noir grape can be found.

40. Name the two important wine produc-ing centers in the Liguria province.

41. Name the four important wines pro-duced in the Emilia-Romagna pro-vince.

42. True/False: Chianti comes only as a white wine.

43. What does the term *abbocato* mean?

44. True/False: Italy exports more wine than any other country in the world.

45. True/False: All wines called "Capri" actually come from Capri.

46. The estate of Duca di Salaparuta produces what Sicilian wine?

47. Name the river in the Piedmont province on which one can find the towns of Alba, Asti and Alessandria.

48. Is the red wine Barbera named for a village or a grape?

49. What grape do the wines of Sassella, Gemello and Inferno have in common?

50. Which red Italian wine is famous for being served in a round flask surrounded by a straw jacket?

51. Name the 19th century prime minister of Italy in whose castle Brolio the classic formulas for the making of Chianti were established.

52. How many types of grapes go into the blend of Chianti according to the classic formula?

53. What is the name of the group of Chiantis *not* put into the usual round flask but into narrow Bordeaux bottles?

54. What is the only firm producing Brunello di Montalcino?

55. What province is the largest wine producer in southern Italy?

56. What is the name of the wine made from the process of hanging grapes and drying them before pressing?

57. True/False: Every region in Italy produces wine.

58. What does the term *frizzante* mean?

59. What is the name of the process in which partially dried grapes are added to the new wine after its fermentation is completed?

60. In what special week, traditionally, is Vin Santo vinified?

61. What wine is distinctive with its amphora-shaped bottles?

62. In what year did Italy pass its "Denominazioni di Origine" laws for controlling place names or denominations of origin?

63. What is the ancient Greek name for Italy's "Land of Wine"?

64. What is the better-known name of the grape Italian vintners call Spanna?

65. In what famous wine region can one find the estate Fontanafredda?

66. True/False: In Barolo, bottles of wine are traditionally kept standing up, unlike all other red wines.

67. True/False: The white wine Tocai, produced in northeast Italy, is named so after its counterpart, the Tokay wine from Hungary.

68. What is the only wine produced in Alto Adige to be ranked D.O.C. (the second highest level of quality)?

69. Of what wine was Michelangelo speaking when he said, "It kisses, it licks, bites, thrusts and stings"?

70. Is the general name Capri given to red or white wine?

71. What is the name of the round, straw-covered flask in which Chianti is served?

72. True/False: The better wines in Italy are, for the most part, found in northern Italy, becoming fewer and far between as one travels south.

73. What three popular wines, among the most exported in Italy, are produced in the province of Veneto?

74. Is Bardolino a red or white wine?

75. Piemonte or Piedmont means "at the foot of the mountains." At the foot of what range of mountains is the province located?

76. What country is the largest market for exported Italian wine?

77. Approximately how much of Italy's exported wine is taken by Germany (in a rough percentage within 10%)?

78. Approximately how much of Italy's exported wine is taken by America? (a rough percentage)?

79. What does the term *vino liquoroso* mean?

80. What does *Imbottoigliato nello stablimento della ditta* mean on a wine label?

81. What does the term *chiaretto* mean?

82. What does *casa vinicola* mean?

83. What does the term *stravecchio* mean?

84. What well-known white wine is produced by five small villages on the coast north of La Spezia in the province of Liguria?

85. Name the "red wine of the Italian Riviera."

86. Is Verdiso red or white?

87. Can the Vincenzan Colli Berici wines be found in red *and* white?

88. What colors are Chiaretto and Bardolino?

89. Are Sorni and Castelle reds or whites?

90. Are Marzemino and Valdadige reds or whites?

91. What is the name of the popular Italian export (a red wine) known as Kalterersee in Germany and Austria where most of it is consumed?

92. What is the name of the well-known white wine produced on the island of Elba?

93. True/False: The world-famous wine produced in the province of Umbria is Lambrusco.

94. Is Cesanese red or white?

95. Is Torgiano red or white?

96. What are the names of Sardinia's two most famous, strong, heavy red wines?

97. Is Vernaccia produced in Sicily or Sardinia?

98. Is Nuragus, a Sardinian wine, red or white?

99. Is the Sicilian Asprinco red or white?

100. Where is Marsala produced?

101. What level of quality do most of Italy's best wines wear on their labels?

102. True/False: The lack of e *garantita* on a label of a premium wine indicates that the wine is, actually, less than first class.

103. Asti Spumante is quite popular. Where in Italy does it come from, and what grape is it made from?

104. What famous Italian winemaker is known for his Taurasi and Lacryma Christi wines?

105. Would you drink an Inferno?

106. Falerno is a modern Italian wine. What is Falernian?

SPAIN/PORTUGAL

1. True/False: Spain is the fourth largest wine producer in the world, ranking behind only Italy, Germany and France.

2. When were the laws passed in Spain that raised the industry's standards throughout the country (similar to the French "Appellation d'Origine Contrôlée")?

3. What is the name of the province situated 100 miles from the French boarder where Spain's most highly acclaimed wines are produced?

4. What major river is Rioja situated on?

5. In what three types of soil are Rioja vines planted?

6. What is the primary black grape of Rioja?

7. What does the term *clarete* mean?

8. True/False: In order to qualify as a *reserva,* a Rioja wine must be aged in a cellar for eight or more years and a *gran reserva* must be aged for at least eight years.

9. What does *bodega* mean?

10. In Allella, white wines are exported under the name "Marfil." What does that term mean?

11. What is the most commonly planted white grape in La Mancha?

12. Where are the wines called Montilla (similar to sherry) found?

13. Majorca is known for production of what type of wine?

14. The Canary Islands primarily produce what type of wine?

15. What is the name of the red wine, formerly known as "Mountain Wine," produced in the southern part of Spain?

16. What is the name of the principal grape in Sherry?

17. What is the name of the town from which the name "Sherry" is derived?

18. True/False: Only Sherry produced in Jerez is *authentic* Sherry.

19. What is the name of the chalky white soil which gives the Palomino grape its distinctive flavor?

20. What town is the capital of the Sherry industry?

21. What are the three main classifications of Sherry?

22. What is the name of the pasty scum that characteristically sets Fino Sherries apart from the others?

23. What is the name of the type of Fino Sherry made only in Sanlúcar de Barrameda?

24. What is Amontillado?

25. What is Oloroso?

26. What is the rarest of the three types of Sherry?

27. What does the term *añada* mean?

28. What is the name of the system based on the principle that a small amount of young wine added to an older wine of the same kind will take on the character of the older wine?

30. Do vintages appear on the labels of Sherries?

31. Are locations of vineyards indicated on the label of bottles of Sherry?

32. What is the mean alcohol range in blended Sherries (in a percent)?

33. What is Portugal's most famous exported wine?

34.   In Portugal, are more reds or whites produced?

35.   In Portugal, are more reds or white exported?

36.   How many official demarcated wine regions are there in Portugal?

37.   What labels are approved wines that satisfy the required standard for each region given?

38.   What does the term *vinhos verdes* mean?

39.   Are *vinhos verdes* so named for their color or their youth?

40.   Name the official demarcated wine regions of Portugal.

41.   True/False: Bucelas is famous for its red wines produced and exported.

42.   What famous Portuguese wine is named after the city of Oporto?

43.   Is Port red, white, or both?

44.   True/False: Port derives its particular character from the fact that it is fortified with Brandy when partially fermented.

45.   True/False: Only wines made from grapes grown in the demarcated area of the Douro Valley region and shipped from Oporto may be sold as Port.

46. True/False: Port is likely to reach maturity after five years of aging.

47. What is the heavy sediment found in Port called?

48. Name the three classifications of wood Ports.

49. Where do the Port shippers submit samples of their vintage wine (can be the product of a single vineyard or a blend of several)?

50. What is *flor*?

51. What is Fino?

52. Amontillado is a type of Sherry, but where did Edgar Allan Poe get his idea for the story "The Cask of Amontillado"?

53. What is a *criadera*?

54. What are the three principal wine producing areas of Spain?

55. What is La Mancha famous for, other than Don Quixote?

56. What is *quinta*?

57. What is Tawny Port?

58. What is Wooded Port?

59. What is Vintage Port?

60. A *vinho do rodo* in Portugal or a

vino espumoso in Spain would be what kind of wine in France?

61. What is a *bastardo*?

62. Beeswing — what is it in the wine world?

GRAPES

1. What is tannin?

2. In what way does tannin benefit a wine?

3. Where besides the skin of the grape is tannin found?

4. Why is there less tannin in white wines?

5. What are the Palomino and Pedro Ximénez used for?

6. What is ampelography?

7. Which German grape is the same as the Spanish Pedro Ximenez?

8. What is the meaning of viticulture?

9. What is the meaning of vinification?

10. What is pruina?

11. What attaches to the skin of the grape, giving it a "frosty" effect?

12. Yeast performs what function?

13. What is another name for Sauvignon Blanc?

14. What is the Bourboulenc used for?

15. What is the Inzolia used for?

16. Where is the Italian black grape Molinara found?

17. Which two Italian wines use the Molinara?

18. What is the German white grape Perle used for?

19. Rosé wines from Anjou use what French black grape?

20. What is the leading white grape of Touraine and Anjou?

21. Where is the Dutchess grape found?

22. Describe the Foch grape.

23. Where is the Isabella grape found?

24. What is the Isabella grape used for?

25. What is the Niagara grape used for?

26. What is the Seyval-Blanc grape used for?

27. What is the Muscat grape used for?

28. What is the Aurora grape used for?

29. Where is the Catawba grape found?

30. What is it used for?

31. What is the most widely grown grape in California?

32. What is the Concord grape used for?

33. What is the Verdelet grape used for?

34. What is another name for the Petite Sirah grape?

35. What is it used for?

36. What is the Pinot St. George grape used for?

37. What is the French Colombard grape used for?

38. What is the Fumé Blanc grape used for?

39. What is the Gamay grape used for?

40. What is the Carignane grape used for?

41. From what grape comes the finest California whites?

42. Mâconnais is made from what grape?

43. What is the only grape that can be used in making French Chablis?

44. Seysel is made from what grape?

45. What grape yields the sparkling wine called Blanquette de Limoux?

46. Colliouse is made from what grape?

47. What grape variety is used for making Muscadet?

48. What is the Mourisco Tinto and what is it used for?

49. Emerald Riesling is made from crossing what two California grapes?

50. What is the Genove?

51. What properties of wine come from the skins of grapes?

52. What is the predominant grape of Saint-Emilion?

53. Where is the Mourvédre found?

54. What wines of that area use the Mourvédre?

55. What grape yields the rosés of Tavel?

56. By French law, how many grape varieties may be used in making red Bordeaux?

57. How many grape varieties may be used in making Beaujolais?

58. What is the Champagne (French) made from white grapes only?

59. What is the meaning of *vendange*?

60. The reds of the Côte d'Or and the

Chalonnais are made from what grape?

61. What area in France uses the Riesling grape to produce dry white wines?

62. What grape produces the most famous white German wines?

63. What grape is combined with the Sémillon to produce the sweet wines of southern Bordeaux?

64. In the Loire Valley, what is this grape (previous answer) referred to as?

65. What wine from Pouilly-sur-Loire uses this grape (previous answer)?

66. What grape yields the red wines of Chinon, St.-Nicholas-de-Bourgueil, and Samur-Champigny?

67. What black grape is blended with Chardonnay to produce champagne?

68. What red wines from Côte d'Or does this grape (previous) yield?

69. What is the most important grape of Graves?

70. Name the white mutations of the Pinot Noir?

71. What is *Botrytis cinerea* commonly referred to as?

72. Which grape found in southern Bordeaux is closely associated with *botrytis*?

73. What types of wines are made from this grape?

74. What is the white grape used in making Champagne?

75. What grape produces the renowned white Burgandies of Côte de Beaune?

76. What is meaning of *gewürz* as in Gewürztraminer?

77. What is the Gewürztraminer called in France?

78. What grape is used in the production of Vouvray?

79. What grape found in Germany can also be affected by *botrytis* to produce sweet white wine?

LABELS

TELL ALL

Most of the major wine producing countries mentioned in this book "tell all" on the label. It's not because the winemakers are models of virtue and good manners. The laws of their particular nation require "full disclosure" on the label.

The German wine laws are the most demanding. If you can decipher the type on the label, every grade of wine, no matter how modest, reveals everything you would want to know about the wine, except how it tastes to you. Every time a German winemaker is caught trying to cut a corner, the laws are revised. Thus, the German wine label depicted here tells you:

1. The region where the grapes were grown (Mosel-Saar-Ruwer)
2. The town and the vineyard (Wehlener-Sonnenuhr)
3. The grape type (Riesling)
4. The quality level (Qualitätswein mit Prädikat)
5. The quality type (Beerenauslese)
6. The winemaker's name (Dr. Bergweiler)
7. The government inspection number (A. P. 2 576 415 1 77)
8. The vintage year (1976)

This is but one example of the many different labels required by German wine law. If you can read a German wine label, you know the quality level of the wine you're buying.

SPÉCIMEN

RÉCOLTE 1978

Grand Vin de Léoville

du Marquis de Las Cases

SAINT-JULIEN

APPELLATION SAINT-JULIEN CONTROLÉE

PROP^ SOCIÉTÉ CIVILE DU CHATEAU LÉOVILLE LAS CASES A SAINT-JULIEN (Gde)

MIS EN BOUTEILLES AU CHATEAU

PRODUCE OF FRANCE   75d

The same goes for the French wine label. One glance at a French wine label and you know what you're buying, from V.D.Q.S. (literal translation: "A wine of limited quality") to a Premier Grand Cru (First Great Growth):

1. Year produced (Récolte 1978)
2. Who produced it (Grand Vin de Léoville du Marquis de Las Cases)
3. Where it was produced (Saint-Julien — a commune in Bordeaux)
4. The body of law that governed its making (Appellation Saint-Julien Controlée
5. Where it was bottled (Mis en Bouteilles au Chateau — it was bottled at the chateau)
6. The nation where it was produced (Produce of France)

As you can see, the French do not reveal as much as the Germans. One must be acquainted with the particular chateau, shipper, region, or labeling laws to be absolutely sure what is in the bottle. For example, the wines from the Pomerol region of Bordeaux contain much more Merlot wine than do the wines from the Margaux region. That's a fact that the wine drinker must know.

On the other hand, in the Alsace region of France, the wine law states that the bottler *must* reveal the name of the grape that produced the wine that's in the bottle. This is not to say that winemakers from other regions can't do it; it's just that they don't:

1. Name of principal grape from which wine is made   (Gewurztraminer)
2. Region from where the wine originated
3. The laws under which the wine was made
4. The producers

Here in the United States, there are federal wine laws and state wine laws. Also, the Bureau of Alcohol, Tobacco and Firearms is supervising a new law that permits winemakers to declare a wine to be produced in a specific region, such as "Alexander Valley." This is similar to the wine laws of France and Germany and usually applies to the premium priced wines.

A UNIQUE
CELEBRATING THE
OF THE GEWÜRZ

VARIETAL ROSÉ
NATURAL PINKISH HUE
TRAMINER GRAPE.

ROSA

VINEYARDS ESTABLISHED 1825

Sebastiani

1983
SONOMA VALLEY
GEWÜRZTRAMINER

PRODUCED AND BOTTLED BY SEBASTIANI VINEYARDS
SONOMA, CALIFORNIA ALC. 12.9% BY VOL.
BONDED WINERY 876

The California wine label reproduced here tells the consumer the following:

1. The producer (Sebastiani)
2. The vintage year (1983)
3. The region in which it was produced (Sonoma Valley)
4. The varietal type of wine (Gewürztraminer)
5. A type of Gewürztraminer (Rosa)
6. Percentage of alcohol in the wine (12.9% by volume)
7. The number of its bonded permit to produce wine (876)

But how about the United States wine labels that read "Burgundy," "Chablis" and other so-called generic names?

Back when our European ancestors were planting their own vineyards in America, it was natural for them to give the wine the name they were most familiar with in the old country. Much to the chagrin of the French, in particular, the United States never signed the Madrid or Lisbon agreements which protect appellations of origin. Therefore, the semi-generic names of Angelica, Burgundy, Claret, Chablis, Champagne, Chianti, Malaga, Marsala, Madeira, Moselle, Port, Rhine Wine (or Hock), Sauterne, Haut Sauterne, Sherry and Tokay do not mean the wine in the bottle is anything like the original wine for which it is named. Also, federal regulations permit the use of regional names such as Napa Valley, Lake Erie Islands and others but they prohibit the use of names such as Pommard, Montrachet, Liebfraumilch or Lacryma Christi. It's "amusin' but confoozin'," as Li'l Abner said, and not likely to be resolved in the near or distant future.

New BATF regulations now permit specific viticultural area designations to appear on United States winemakers' labels as they conform to specific criteria defined by the BATF.

There are four official categories of Italian wine that have been determined under the national and EEC (European Economic Community) policies:

1. Denominazione di Origine Controllata (DOC)
2. Denominazione di Origine Controllata e Garantitia (DOCG)
3. Vini Tipici
4. Vini da Tavola

Italy, literally the vineyard of Europe, has managed by the passage of these laws to bring respectability to some of the finest wines the world has known.

Most of the wines imported into the United States are DOC wines, indicated by a seal which is generally placed on the neck of the bottle or on the seal that covers the cork. DOC means that the wine was made under

specified conditions of terrain from specifically determined amounts of clearly defined grape varieties, and that the vinification has been subject to control. For example, Chianti wine must contain three different types of wine according to the formula set down by Baron Ricasoli in 1872: Sangiovese, Canaiolo and Malvasia. But, to permit the winemaker to use his own judgment and style, the percentages can vary just as long as all three are present.

Spanish wines, becoming more and more popular in the United States, are made under grower association laws. Portugese wines, in particular Port, is rigidly controlled by both the government and a producers association.

Port can only be made from grapes grown in the specially delimited Douro Valley. The types are: Ruby, Tawny, Crusted, White, Late-bottled Vintage Port and Vintage Port.

Sheldon Wasserman, in his book, "Guide to Fortified Wines" (Marlborough Press, Morganville, NJ), states flatfootedly, "Vintage Port, the greatest of all Port (and of all fortified wine), is the epitome of a bottled Port." Vintage Port is the Port of a single vintage that has been declared a vintage by the shipper between January 1 and September 30 of the second year and June 30 of the third year after the harvest. The label must specify the year of the harvest and carry the word "vintage." The only other type of Port which is allowed to carry the word "vintage" with the date of the harvest on the bottle is Late-bottled Vintage Port.

Madeira, also a product of Portugal, is produced in four styles: Sercial, Verdelho, Bual (or Boal) and Malmsey. Sercial is pale gold in color, dry with a slightly mild, bitter aftertaste: a good aperitif. Verdelho is dry to sweet and goes well with cream soups. Bual is rich, splendid with fruit, fruitcake, nuts and blue cheeses. Malmsey, a deep-colored, lust-rous wine is rare and the best of the four types. A marvelous dessert wine, it is a custom of the island to serve half an avocado with a bit of Malmsey poured into the center for an appetizer.

PEOPLE, PLACES AND THINGS

Identify

People, Places and Things

Picture 1

Picture 2

Picture 3

a

b

Picture 4

Picture 5

Picture 6

Picture 7

Picture 8

Picture 9

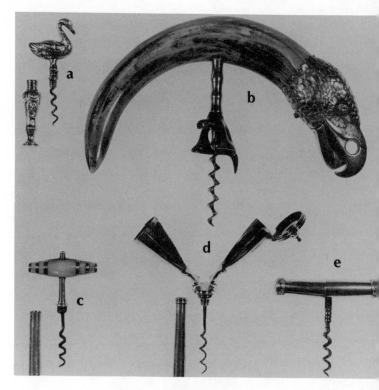

Picture 10

ANSWERS

GENERAL

1. Samuele Sebastiani

2. Italy

3. Italy

4. Bottling before fermentation is complete

5. Brandy

6. Dry, unfortified sweet, fortified, and sparkling

7. Wines become brown and lose sugar

8. 6.0 litres (8 bottles)

9. 4.5 litres (6.0 bottles)

10. 1.5 litres (2 bottles)

11. 9.0 litres (12 bottles)

12. Grape louse, perhaps the grape vine's worst enemy. *Phylloxera* nearly destroyed the European wine industry in the 1870s.

13. *Vitis vinifera*

14. Dom Pérignon

15. Benedictine monk

16. Blindness

17. U.S.A.

18. Thomas Jefferson on a Château Margaux

19. Claret

20. Pablo Picasso

21. Baron Philippe de Rothschild

22. Varietals

23. Generic

24. 52°-56° F

25. The cork dries out and the wine evaporates.

26. Growth of fungus

27. Wine "breathes" through the cork; thus, standing odors will be absorbed into the wine.

28. The wine throws off its sediment too soon.

29. 75%

30. Purple

31. Green

32. Desserts and pastries

33. False

34. Metric

35. Hectolitres per hectare

36. 100

37. 133

38. 2.47

39. 160 and 15 (these amounts vary with the type of wine)

40. Three days

41. Two to three months

42. 2 1/2 inches

43. Hollow is the best type — it takes a firm hold within the cork and minimizes cork breakage.

44. The wine butler

45. A cork "extractor"

46. If you pierce the cork in the exact center, the actual pressure line will end up at the side.

47. It separates the wine from any sediment which, if suspended in the wine, can cause a bitter taste.

48. Two to three hours

49. Allow wine to flow down inside the neck of the decanter.

50. All wines need some aereation to reach their full flavor.

51. True — the breathing time minimizes its acidity and tannin.

52. The White Chalk Cliffs on the English Channel coast

53. Cabernet Sauvignon, generally

54. True — a magnum is the ideal size and half bottles age faster than fifths.

55. Champagne, sparkling or still white wines

56. Sherry, Marsala and Sauternes

57. Port, Sherry, Madeira and Brandy

58. No, it is only important that the wine remain in contact with the base of the cork.

59. True

60. A 1771 claret, estate not known

61. .55%

62. 18-24%

63. "Selected," a *Prädikat* wine (German)

64. Wine expert (production, care, handling)

65. French sparkling wine not made in Champagne

66. Still wines made in the Champagne region

67. 1822 Château Lafite

68. The St. Jude's Children's Research Hospital

69. Ullage

70. 1981

71. Chicago

72. Four

73. 1981

74. Patrick Grubb

75. June, 1981

76. Robert Mondavi and Baron Philippe de Rothschild, owner of Château Mouton-Rothschild

77. Meadowood Country Club in St. Helena, California

78. The labels were banned by the Bureau of Alcohol, Tobacco and Firearms as "obscene and indecent."

79. A nude women reclining on a hillside

80. Sotheby's Wine Department

81. The coupe and the flute

82. Upright, with tissue paper across to prevent dust accumulation. If stored upside down, moisture sometimes appears in the bowl, and the glass can pick up the smell of the shelf.

83. Heublein, Christie's and Sotheby's

84. 1969

85. Heublein

86. Clarity, size, shape and breakage

87. The tulip glass

88. 8-10 oz.

89. The tulip wine glass has a: a) rounder bowl, b) more extreme curve of the inward rim, c) larger capacity

90. Louis XIV

91. The white wine glass has a: a) smaller capacity, b) long stem to avoid warming the wine with hand heat, c) moderate curve of the inward rim

92. The Copita

93. True (as a general rule)

94. 40°-45° F

95. 46°-52° F

96. 48°-52° F

97. 60°-65° F

98. A flat, shallow, silver wine-taster's cup widely used in Burgundy for tasting wine

99. 2/3 ice to 1/3 cold water

100. No more than 1/2, no less than 1/3

101. Roquefort

102. All are fermented.

103. Measure of the strength of acidity

104. The lower the figure, the more acid strength

105. -2.8-3.8

106. Warren Winiarski (Stag's Leap Wine Cellars) and Carl Doumani (Stag's Leap Winery)

107. 1966

108. Christina Crawford, author of *Mommie Dearest*

109. New York, Boston, Chicago, Houston and Los Angeles

110. A wine that has taken on the flavor of a bad cork

111. Robert Mondavi

112. Port

113. A sweet, fortified wine from the island of Cyprus

114. In French, "growth"

115. The French term from which the English term "demi-john" is derived; it is a large glass bottle of indeterminate size and usually covered with wicker used for storing and transporting wine.

116. Genesis (9:21)

117. 50.7 ounces

118. A red Hungarian wine known as Bull's Blood

119. Furmint

120. Sweetened Oloroso Sherry, bottled in Bristol, England

121. Champagne comes in ten differently sized bottles ranging from a split (6.7 oz.) to a Nebuchadnezzar (540.93 oz.)

122. Nothing except size. They're all barrels in which you store or age wine.

123. Madeira

124. Labrusca (native American)

125. According to wine historian Charles Sullivan, the Zinfandel

126. The heavy, coarse sediment which young wines throw in the barrel before they are ready for racking

127. Up to 100

128. Wermut, from the German meaning wormwood

129. Port, Sherry, Madeira and Marsala

130. Angelica, named for the city of Los Angeles

131. He was supposed to have said, "It tastes of sinners."

132. Ohio

133. "Drink no longer water but use a little wine for thy stomach's sake and thine often infirmities."

134. Petit Chablis is a wine made from grapes grown in less favored vineyards of the Chablis section of Burgundy.

135. 1971

136. $5,000.00

137. A Bordeaux from Château Lafite Rothschild, 1846.

138. $465.00 for a bottle of the same wine

139. Heublein Wine Auction

140. Michael Broadbent, M.W.

141. Master of Wine

142. London, England

143. Atlanta International, Los Angeles County Fair, Orange County, River-

side County, San Francisco Fair, San Jose Mercury News, West Coast Wine Competition (Reno, NV) and Vintage Magazine Awards

144. Cabernet Sauvignon, Pinot Noir, Chardonnay, Riesling and Gewürztraminer

145. Nebbiolo and Barbera

146. Each is made from the Nebbiolo grape.

147. Small, seedless berries found in a bunch of otherwise normal grapes resulting from incomplete pollinization

148. A wine that is cloudy, has an unpleasant odor and an "off" taste

149. Carruades du Château Lafite-Rothschild — not made since 1966

150. St. Helena, California

151. It has an earthy, sometimes unpleasant taste.

152. 1782

153. Not Fr. Junipero Serra, as popularly believed. Rather, two of his fellow Franciscans, Frs. Pablo de Mugartegui and Gregorio Amurrio.

154. Mission San Juan Capistrano, California

155. From a *vinifera* grape now known as

the Mission grape. It produced a sweet wine used for religious ceremonies.

156. Sam J. Sebastiani, Sebastiani Vineyards, Sonoma, CA

157. In 1838 by George Yount

158. Buena Vista

159. Just east of Sonoma, where Haraszthy settled in 1856

160. Los Angeles, Anaheim and Sonoma

161. Mirassou Vineyards

162. 1889. Some French shippers were accused of importing California wines to France and re-shipping the wine to the United States labeled as French wine from Bordeaux.

163. Kew Gardens, England

164. *Vitis rupestris,* a native American grape root stock

165. Carl Reiner. The "li'l ole winemaker" was Mel Brooks.

166. Maine, 1851

167. .0164 gallons per capita

168. Alicante Bouschet, a thick-skinned red grape that can survive the rigors of rail transportation

169. The autumn of 1933

170. He discovered the micro-organisms

that cause grape juice to ferment (yeast).

171. 155 times

172. Ten times

173. Bacchus

174. In 1781 at Château Lafite Rothschild.

175. Tartaric, malic and citric

176. In 1562 by French Huguenots in Jacksonville, Florida

177. 42

178. Maui Blanc, made from pineapples and produced by Tedeschi Vineyards

179. The Pennsylvania Wine Co., Ltd., of Spring Mill, Pennsylvania, which opened in 1793

180. Jean-Louis Vinges, a Frenchman from Bordeaux who planted the vineyard in 1833

181. Six: North Coast, Sacramento Valley, Central Valley, San Joaquin Valley, South Coast and San Luis Obispo

182. Five

183. The number of degree days or temperature variations: in this case, a minimum of 1,500 degree days

184. Georges de Latour founded Beaulieu Vineyards.

185. Bernard Portet

186. Dominique Portet is the proprietor of Taltarni Winery in the Yarra Valley of Australia.

187. Pat Paulsen

188. Tom and Dick Smothers

189. Stag's Leap Wine Cellars

190. Warren Winiarski

191. Domaine Chandon

192. Francis Ford Coppola

193. Pleasant Valley Wine Co., Hammondsport, New York

194. The Christian Brothers

195. Brother Timothy

196. Brother Timothy owns one of the world's finest collection of corkscrews.

197. "...the wine is bottled poetry."

198. 105 years old

199. Father Duran of the Santa Barbara Mission, 1833

200. Don Mariano Guadalupe Vallejo, a Mexican general. A memorial plaque can be seen in the town of Sonoma's beautiful park.

201. The 1830 catalogue of viticulturist William Prince of Long Island, New York. He called it the "Black Zinfandel."

202. Black St. Peter

203. Paul Draper of Ridge Vineyards credits Captain Frederick W. Macondray and J.W. Osborne of Napa.

204. Region I, the northerly most region

205. Eight: White, Rosé, Nouveau, Early Maturing, Late Maturing, Late Picked, Late Harvest and Port

206. Vino Santo (holy wine)

207. Charbono

208. Syrah

209. *Pierre a fusil*

210. "You should sooner forget to kiss your wife on returning home than to leave a vacancy in your barrel."

211. Louis Wente of Livermore, California

212. Chateau d'Yquem in 1878

213. Fruity, green-olive, faintly herbaceous

214. Sémillon

215. Pineau de la Loire, White Pinot and Vouvray

216. Burger

217. Nicholas Longworth of Ohio

218. Catawba

219. Benjamin Davis Wilson, a Tennessean by birth, for whom Mt. Wilson was named

220. In the transfer process, the second fermentation takes place in the bottle; in the *charmat* process, the second fermentation takes place in a steel tank.

221. A fortified wine made from the Pinot Noir grape, then aged in oak for a brief period

222. Hagafen Cellars, Napa Valley

223. Yes, canon law requires that the wine be made exclusively from grapes and it cannot contain more than 20% alcohol.

224. Thomas Hardy (1840-1928) wrote *Notes on Vineyards in America* in 1885.

225. Any grape or number of grapes the producer cares to blend

226. 85%

227. The wine has a combination of sweetness, alcohol and glycerol and lacks the proper acidity.

228. 24%

229. It means that the wine in the bottle was made entirely on the premises

from grapes grown on its own land in the same viticulturally defined area.

230. 1795 by Samuel Henshall, an English parson

231. F.A. Weinke, a German engineer, in 1883

232. Because the cork can be pulled and replaced literally without detection

233. "The invention of the cork is the most important event in the history of fine wine."

234. Fifth after Italy, France, Spain and Russia

235. 27th

236. France with 22.7 gallons per capita per year

237. French Colombard

238. 81%

239. As of the end of 1983, 639

240. 445

241. Napa

242. Number 1. E. & J. Gallo of Modesto, California produces an estimated 62 million cases of all types of wine as of the end of 1983.

243. White wine accounts for 61% of the total wine consumed.

244. Cold Duck

245. From the German *Kalte Ende* meaning "cold end"

246. 7% or 11,000,000 people

247. The professional by far; 4.8 gallons per person vs. 1.6 gallons per person for the blue-collar family

248. The northeast and the west

249. The French prefer red wines by 86%; Americans prefer whites by 61%.

250. The show is "Falcon Crest"; the home was built by Tiburcio Parrot.

251. The Revenue Act of 1789 imposed a tax on imported wine.

252. During the Civil War in 1862, a supposedly temporary tax of 5¢ a gallon was imposed on all domestic wines. The tax was abolished in 1865.

253. Missouri

254. Sight, taste and smell

255. "Not since lunch."

256. 50′ north, 20′ south, both hemispheres

257. Broadbent rates the vintage year 1910 as an unprecedented disaster.

258. No, a vintage year is declared by the majority of the "grande marque" houses, although a maverick producer can declare his own vintage year.

259. Exposure to oxygen — wine will have a heavy, baked smell

260. Bodrog

261. The sediment from the wine that takes years to settle. It is the one wine that must be stored upright.

262. Puttonyos (Poo-tawn-yawsh). Five puttonyos is the sweetest.

263. A pleasant, dry white wine made from the Sauvignon Blanc grape

264. Madeira, developed by a man named Habisham from Savannah, Georgia

265. No, it's actually a beer. It is made by cleaning, steaming and then fermenting rice, a grain.

266. A basic red wine which, when fermenting, has the grape skins removed so that only a touch of the color is retained

267. A. D. 1680

268. Methyl anthranilate

269. Literally, "top of the barrel." Generally, this refers to the best of the wines.

270. Greek wine flavored with pine resin, a habit developed in ancient times when wine jugs were sealed with pine pitch

271. Supposedly the first wine that was made. Shah Djemsheed of Persia kept grapes by his bed. When they fermented, he marked it poison but a harem girl tasted it, pronounced it "superb," and she and the Shah lived happily ever after.

272. It celebrates the Hebrew Yaykin, the wine which Noah made after the flood.

273. Usually referred to as a wine that has yet to develop its bouquet, found in immature fine wines.

274. Excess tannin and acid, mainly tannin, usually found in young red wines

275. Pleasant Valley Wine Company, Hammondsport, New York

276. Great Western

277. The Baltimore Sun; Philip Wagner

278. Rev. William Bostwick

279. Charles Fournier

280. In a garden in a convent in Quebec, Canada

281. If the buyer combined the yeast and the grape juice, ". . . this will in turn become wine which would be illegal."

282. "Wine is constant proof that God loves us and loves to see us happy."

283. The Patwins

284. Ta-La-Ha-Lu-Si, which meant "beautiful land"

285. Mexico, the United States and Russia

286. Valley of the Moon. You can see it today in beautiful downtown Sonoma.

287. George Yount in 1831, a native of South Carolina for whom the town of Yountville is named

288. Charles Krug. The winery is still in existence.

289. Peter Mondavi, brother of Robert

290. 4,252,000 gallons

291. Port

292. Johannisberg Riesling

293. Beerenauslese

294. Chicama Vineyard, owned and operated by George Mathiessen on Martha's Vineyard, Massachusetts

295. In Napa Valley, owned and operated by Joe Heitz

296. Biturica, named after the Celtic tribe that lived in the region

297. Bouquet — 4 points out of the total of 20 for the perfect wine

298. The highest rating on the Hedonic scale is 9 points, which means "I like it extremely well."

299. From ancient Greek — "Drinking together"

300. The symposiarch. Like your friendly bartender, he could shut things off if they got too boisterous.

301. A wine drink created by Hippocrates, the father of modern medicine, composed of wine sweetened with honey and flavored with cinammon

302. The Gauls, circa 51 B.C., in defense of Uxellodunum. They were filled with inflammable matter.

303. August Sebastiani's 1941 Case de Sonoma. About 500 cases are on the market.

304. Approximately 5%

305. Shampanskoe

306. Thomas Jefferson, the third president of the United States, and John Winthrop, the first governor of Massachusetts, who set aside Governor's Island in Boston Harbor (since leveled to extend Logan Airport) for grape cultivation

307. Virginia Dare, a scuppernong wine made famous by "Captain" Paul Garret

308. Moet et Chandon for their Champagnes and Veuve Cliquot Ponsardin, another "Grand Marque" Champagne house

309. Isabella (1816), Lenoir (1892) and Herbemont (1820s)

310. Henry Wadsworth Longfellow:
Very good in its way is the Verzenay,
Or the Sillery soft and creamy;
But the Catawba wine
Has a taste more divine,
More dulcet, delicious and dreamy.

311. The French wine Coca, circa 1880s

312. About 8,000

313. Pinot Blanc

314. Weissburgunder

315. Sylvaner, Emerald Riesling and Muller-Thurgau

316. No. It is related to the Chauche Gris, a French grape found in Vienne and Charente.

317. The Italian Tyrol, south of Lake Caldaro

318. The Palomino, one of the great grapes of Jerez, Spain

319. Almaden, founded in 1847 by Etienne Thée

320. Charles Lefranc

321. Paul Masson

322. André Tchelistcheff, formerly Beaulieu's winemaker and now consultant to many wineries in California

323. Green Hungarian

324. 28 red varieties; 20 white varieties

325. Dynamite

326. Manzanilla, a type of sherry

327. Sherry

328. American bourbon distillers buy the barrels back because the Sherry lends a depth of flavor to the better bourbon whiskies.

329. Cato the Censor (234-149 B.C.)

330. To help maintain the tartaric acid in the wine and to give the wine better balance

331. From the Spanish word *sacar* — to take out or take away or to export

332. John Woodhouse, a Liverpool, England merchant, in 1773

333. Joshua and Caleb

334. No, but a change of scenery does. The Spatburgunder in Germany is the Pinot Noir of France, but it doesn't make the same fine wine in Germany.

335. Wine running freely from the residue after fermentation or from pressed wine at the first light pressing

336. Wine made from the pressing of the residues after the regular wine has been made

337. Lebanon

338. A tube or pipette for withdrawing wine from a cask

339. A method of training vines

340. A wine so harsh that it can, supposedly, choke the drinker

341. A winebroker

342. A cask used for aging and storing Rheingau wines

343. The former is a wine district in Spain; the latter a wine district in Argentina.

344. Mareotic wine, a fine wine of ancient Egypt

345. Greece (a red, sweet dessert wine)

346. No, it is also a wine produced in Algiers.

347. The wiring that holds down the cork in a Champagne bottle

348. A small cask, one-eighth the capacity of a pipe. The octave ranges in capacity from 14 to 21 gallons.

349. They are three different terms, Latin, French and German, for the beneficial fungus that penetrates grapes without breaking the skin and concentrates the sugars.

350. A "hat" of thick solids that forms on the grape juice (must) while it is fermenting in the vat

351. White, the better to see the true color of the wine

352. "Buy on bread, sell on cheese."

353. Tart on the palate; vinegary on the nose

354. All the elements that go into making a good wine are in balance or proper proportion (mainly sugar and acid).

USA

1. Spanish missionaries

2. Chardonnay and Johannisberg Riesling

3. Count Agoston Haraszthy

4. *Phylloxera* — a disease that spread throughout Europe prior to devastating American wineries

5. 1865-1890

6. By grafting with vines that had an apparent immunity to the disease

7. Commonwealth Winery, Plymouth, Massachusetts

8. Robert Louis Stevenson

9. Count Agoston Haraszthy

10. Plenty

11. Cabernet Sauvignon

12. Bordeaux wines are blends (Cabernet Sauvignon and Merlot, etc.), while the Cabernet Sauvignon is a "varietal" (one grape, very little blending).

13. French Colombard, Chenin Blanc, Chardonnay, White Riesling, Sauvignon Blanc and the Gewürztraminer

14. Zinfandel

15. White Riesling

16. De Loach 1983 — White Zinfandel

17. New York

18. Sparkling wines, fortified wines and dry white wines

19. Concord and Elvira

20. Finger Lakes district

21. Hudson Valley and North Fork (Long Island)

22. Great Western Winery

23. Taylor Wine

24. Coca-Cola Company

25. America's leading producer of dessert wines and premium sparkling wines

26. Northeast Vineyard

27. Johnson Estate Wines

28. Chateau Esperanza Winery

29. W.S. Taylor, grandson of Walter Taylor

30. Dr. Konstantin Frank

31. Successfully cultivating *vinifera* wines in New York

32. Crosses between European and American varieties

33. Seyve-Villard, Maréchal Foch and Baco Noir

34. Concord and Elvira

35. Pinot Noir, Riesling and Chardonnay

36. French-American hybrid grape used in red wines from New York and Canada

37. Champagne

38. French hybridist known for producing the Seyval Blanc

39. American white grape — commonly used for sweet wines

40. Maréchal Foch

41. Gold Seal

42. Chautauqua

43. Catawba

44. Brights

45. Started Boordy Vineyards, one of the first to promote French/American hybrids

46. Aurora (French/American hybrid)

47. Château St. Chapelle

48. Château St. Michelle

49. Argentina

50. Wine produced and bottled at the same vineyard

51. True

52. 1919

53. Produced sacramental wines and sold grapes as fruit and juices

54. 1933

55. 1956

56. To prove that American wines were equal to the best of Europe

57. Kosher wines

58. Concord

59. Ephraim Wales Bull, 1854

60. Rabbi's *hechsher* seal

61. Leo Star, founder of Monarch Wine Company

62. Manischewitz

63. Mogen David Wine

64. Shield of David

65. Joseph Chapman, 1824

66. Major John Adlum

67. Rev. W. Bostwick, 1829

68. 1934

69. 1936

70. University of California at Davis

71. 1950

72. Unfermented fruit or berry juice

73. The French is a rich, sweet dessert wine while the California version is usually drier and can be made from any grape the vintner chooses. Note also that the California version is spelled without the final "s."

74. Late owner of Story Hill

75. Coca-Cola Company

76. Napa Valley

77. California red grape of Italian origin

78. Robert Mondavi/Baron Philippe de Rothschild

79. Cabernet Sauvignon

80. The approach to the main entrance is by cable car.

81. Cabernet Sauvignon, Sauvignon Blanc, Merlot and Chardonnay

82. James and Barbara Spaulding

83. UVAS Valley

84. 95%

85. 75%

86. 51%/75%

87. 85%

88. Frank Bartholomew (United Press International)

89. Beringer Vineyards

90. False. Both are required.

91. Wine is bottled by the winery stated but produced by some other vineyard.

92. Inglenook and Franciscan

93. Cecil De Loach

94. Robert Mondavi

95. Semillon

96. Cribari & Sons, on the third floor of the Starret Liegh building

97. Mr. B. Cribari's grandson Kenneth was on Cribari's Sonnie Boy label until removed by order of the old A.T.O.

FRANCE

1. Half bottles used in Bordeaux

2. Never

3. The only way that an owner can guarantee the authenticity of his wine

4. No

5. *Phylloxera vastatrix* (root louse)

6. United States

7. European grape rootstalks were grafted with American vines and rootstalks.

8. Château Lafite 1797 (still aging)

9. There is none.

10. Merlot

11. Wines made from the juice of any white grape

12. A subdivision of a district

13. Four

14. Château d'Yquem

15. Premier Grand Cru Classé A

16. Premier Grand Cru Classé B

17. Sauternes

18. Barsac

19. Premier Grand Cru

20. Andy Warhol

21. Visit of England's Queen Mother

22. Château Mouton-Rothschild

23. Château Haut-Brion, Graves

24. Pauillac, St. Estéphe, St. Julien, Margaux and Graves

25. Pomerol

26. No one is allowed to taste this wine until *after* it is bottled.

27. *Négociant*

28. Domoto

29. *Récolte*

30. 24

31. Médoc, Graves, St. Emilion, Pomerol and Sauternes

32. Médoc, Graves, St. Emilion and Pomerol

33. White, sweet dessert wines

34. Haut-Médoc (High Médoc) and Médoc (used to be called low Médoc)

35. Haut-Médoc

36. Communes

37. Entre-Deux-Mers

38. Gironde River

39. Dordogne River (North) and Garonne River (South)

40. Cabernet Sauvignon

41. Merlot, Cabernet Franc and Malbe

42. Sémillon

43. Ausonius

44. Sauvignon Blanc, Sémillon and Muscadelle

45. Château Lafite, Château Latour and Château Mouton

46. Only one: Château Margaux

47. Claret

48. The marriage of Eleanor of Aquitaine and Henry II (the Bordeaux area was part of her dowry)

49. A Bordelais word for both the winery and cellar

50. Person responsible for the wine from the moment it is made until it is sold

51. Machine that tears off the stalks and splits the grapes

52. Solid remnants which rise to the top of the must after fermentation

53. Châteaux Pichon Longueville-Baron and Pichon Longueville-Lalaude

54. Châteaux Pontet-Canet and Lynch-Bages

55. Clarence Dillon, former American ambassador to France

56. Château Cheval Blanc

57. The wines must be made by the *méthode champenoise* (individual bottle fermentation).

58. Vouvray and Saumur, Pouilly-Fumé

59. Cuvée close, sparkling wine made in bulk (tank as opposed to individual bottles)

60. Southeastern corner of France

61. The Greeks

62. Côtes-de-Provence

63. Palette, Cassis, Bandol and Bellet

64. Marseille

65. Said to have been named by Julius Caesar

66. Rosé

67. Châteauneuf-du-Pape

68. Blanquette de Limoux

69. Jurancon

70. 1930s

71. Place of origin of the wine

72. Wines for drinking in a cafe

73. Châteauneuf-du-Pape (15%)

74. Professor Saintsbury

75. Bourgogne

76. Chablis and Côte d' Or

77. Côte Chalonnoise, Mâconnais and Beaujolais

78. Côte de Nuits (north) and Côte de Beaune (south)

79. Chardonnay

80. Gamay

81. Pinot Noir

82. Pinot Noir

83. Gamay

84. White Aligoté

85. Pinot Noir and Gamay

86. Monasteries

87. The vineyards were taken from the Church and parceled, then sold to the people.

88. Proprietors who bottled their own wine

89. *Mis au Domaine*

90. Grand Cru (most distinguished) and Premier Cru

91. Grand Cru — Montrachet, Chambertin; Premier Cru — Beaune Les Gréves, Vosne-Romanée, Premier Cru Les Vougeot

92. World's northern-most area which is capable of producing excellent red wine

93. "Vineyard" (literal meaning is "climate"). The use of *clima* reflects the dynamic variation of sun, rain, winds, etc.

94. The custom of inheritance, where a given parcel (vineyard) is divided amongst the offspring

95. The area is "hilly"; thus, two vineyards which are side by side may

have different amounts of exposure to the sun and wind.

96. One to two years

97. Bourgogne

98. White and red, (Chardonnay or Pinot Noir)

99. Bourgogne Aligoté

100. White

101. Grand Cru

102. Fixin

103. Gevrey-Chambertin

104. All bear the name *Chambertin;* some followed by a hyphen, then the village

105. Less tannin

106. Four

107. Clos de Vougeot (Grand Cru)

108. Many different people

109. Vosne-Romaneé

110. 31

111. Grand Cru carries the name of the vineyard, Premier Cru carries the name of the village, then the vineyard

112. Nuits-Saint-Georges

113. Corton

114. Beaune

115. Light and fruity, they should be drunk young.

116. Beaujolais, Beaujolais Supérior, Beaujolais-Villages and Cru Beaujolais

117. Beaujolois Superior has one degree more alcohol.

118. One of 39 designated villages

119. North Haut Beaujolois (one of nine villages — Brouilly, Chénas, Chiroubles, Côte de Brouilly, Fleuire, Julieńas, Morgon, Moulin-á-Vent, Saint-Armour)

120. November 15

121. 9%

122. A term used in Burgundy to identify the Chardonnay grape

123. Sevein River

124. Four

125. Grand Cru Chablis

126. Premier Cru

127. Grand Cru always names the vineyard.

128. Seven (Vaudésir, Valmur, Grenouilles,

Les Clos, Les Pseuses, Blanchots and Bourgros)

129. Mâcon

130. Montrachet, Meursault and Corton-Charlemagne

131. Bourgogne Passe-Toût-Grains

132. Reds or rosés (Pinots or Gamay)

133. Bourgogne Grand Ordinaire and Bourgogne Ordinaire

134. Northeast France, bordered by the Vosges Mountains (west) and the Rhine River (east).

135. Names the grape variety as opposed to the vineyard or village

136. Alsace was annexed by Germany after the Franco-Prussian War (1871) until the end of World War One (1918).

137. Green

138. *Flute* (slim, long necked)

139. Grand Cru

140. Blended wines

141. All of the wines must originate from the same source

142. A blended Alsatian wine from two or more noble grapes

143. Usually one cannot tell because these labels do not reveal the different grape varieties, but usually *Sylvaner* is used in the blend

144. Müller-Thurgau, Chasselas and Knipperlé

145. The wine must contain more than 11% alcohol.

146. A blend of both noble and common varieties of grapes

147. Alsatian rosé (pink wine)

148. Pinot Noir

149. Riesling

150. Dry and fruity

151. Gewürztraminer

152. Generally accepted as the third in quality of Alsatian wines

153. Pinot Gris

154. No, other than the belief that the grape variety originally came from the Tokaji district of Hungary

155. German wines are much more concerned with sweetness, while Alsatian wines are made for strength as an accompaniment of fine food.

156. Grape variety

157. Late-picked grapes for added sweetness and strength

158. Word given to restaurants serving Alsatian food

159. The producer has pronounced this particular wine as one of his best. This term is not sanctioned by law — it merely means that the vintner stakes his reputation on it.

160. Wine of Alsace, the only official appellation of the region

161. German wines tend to be sweeter.

162. Edelzwicker

163. Lyon (north) and Avignon (south)

164. Site of the ancient Palace of the Popes

165. Clement V

166. "New castle of the pope" (summer castle built by Clement V)

167. Châteauneuf-du-Pape

168. Avignon

169. Châteauneuf-du-Pape

170. There is none — a blend of many as 13 grape varieties are used

171. It is a the most frequently used grape in the Rhône Valley

172. Thomas Jefferson

173. Châteauneuf-du-Pape

174. Côtes du Rhône and Côtes du Rhône Villages

175. Terraces of vineyards stacked on a hill overlooking the Rhône (the Romans grew wine in this area)

176. Robust, full-bodied and assertive (manly)

177. Stony, granular soil and hot, rather dry summers

178. Grenache (used for blending)

179. Grape used for Château Grillet white wines

180. Condrieu

181. Only seventeen

182. Vineyards of Côte Rôtie, northern Côtes du Rhône

183. Individual appellations (Côte Rôtie, St. Joseph, Hermitage, etc.)

184. Wines made from vineyards in Cornas or steep hillsides where the sun has maximum exposure on the soil

185. Semi-sparkling wine from the Drôuce River area.

186. Rosés (some say, the best of France)

187. Wine skins are removed after pressing when the correct shade of pink appears.

188. Grenache

189. Lirac and Chusclan

190. A fortified, sweet dessert wine

191. Provence

192. Burgundy shaped bottle

193. Domaine de Mont-Redon, Château Vaudieu, Château-Fortia, Château Maucoil and Clos Saint Pierre

194. Wines from Hermitage

195. Crozes-Hermitage

196. Pouilly-Fumé

197. Dry and crisp

198. Sauvignon Blanc

199. Chasselas

200. Sancerre

201. Pouilly-Fumé is made from the Sauvignon grape (Loire Valley); Pouilly-Fuisse is made from the Pinot Chardonnay (Burgundy).

202. Nautes

203. Muscadet

204. Saumur (white sparkling)

205. Muscadet

206. Appellation Muscadet, Muscadet de Se'vre-et-Maim and Muscadet des Coteaux de la Loire

207. 12%

208. Anjou

209. Cabernet Franc

210. The middle Loire region, around the city of Tours

211. Azay-le-Rideau, Ambiose and Mesland

212. Chenin Blanc and the red Cabernet Franc

213. Vouvray

214. Dry, sweet, still and sparkling

215. Chenin Blanc

216. Mousseux (made by the Champagne method)

217. Most are best drunk while young. The sweeter wines, particularly those that have been effected by *botrytis cinerea,* can be aged for 20-30 years or more.

218. Chinon and Bourgueil (Cabernet Franc grape both of Touraine)

219. Saumur

220. Sparkling and white

221. Château du Nozet

222. Lynch. The châteaus are Lynch-Bages (fifth growth, Pauillac) and Lynch-Moussas (fifth growth)

223. Kirwan, who came from Galway like the Lynches. Château Kirwan is a third growth, Margaux.

224. I thought you'd never ask. Listed as Grand Bourgeois wines are Château MacCarthy and a Cru Bourgeois, Château MacCarthy-Moula.

225. November 15th

226. Saint Vincent. His feast day is January 22.

227. Ugni Blanc

228. Dessert. Beaume de Venise is a Muscat wine from the Rhône region of France. And it is good.

229. Clerget-Buffet et Fils and Raoul Clerget et Fils are, respectively, the sixth and seventh oldest continuous businesses in the world.

230. The invasion of the *phylloxera* louse, which destroyed French vineyards and cost the French more than the indemnity forced upon them by Bismark for having lost the war (5,000,000,000

francs to the Germans; 10,000,000,000
francs loss from the root louse).

231. 60

232. Bernadine monks of Citeaux

233. Navel

234. Charles VI in 1415

235. Santenay

236. "Never let a wine unworthy of you
pass your lips" and "Never drink too
much — it is inadvisable and nothing
to be proud about."

237. Etiquette

238. The Rhône — one of the best communes of the Côte du Rhône

239. 17 ounces

240. 1973

241. A fungicide spray used to fight
mildew in the vineyards

CHAMPAGNE

1. The use of the cork to seal the bottle

2. White Chardonnay

3. Pinot Noir and Pinot Meunier

4. Blanc de Blanc

5. Dark skins are removed before fermentation.

6. All Champagnes are blended wines.

7. Blend of wines from one specific year.

8. Non-vintage Champagne

9. Two

10. A solution of sugar and yeast used in the second stage of fermentation

11. The wine is bottled with a small amount of *liqueur de tirage* and, as fermentation starts, the resulting carbon dioxide cannot escape.

12. When the bottles are tilted during the second fermentation to allow the sediment to collect in the neck

13. The neck of the bottle is frozen and, as the cork is removed, the gases push out the plug of ice and sediment.

14. It must have the distinctive mushroom shape, it must be wired, and it must be printed with the word "Champagne."

15. No perceptible sweetness

16. Very slightly sweet

17. Sweet

18. Very sweet

19. As an aperitif, usually

20. At dessert

21. Shallow, wide brimmed glasses dissipate the bubbles.

22. A white wine made from any black grapes

23. A non-vintage wine using grapes from more than one year

24. A wine of less effervescence (sugar was added just prior to the second fermentation)

25. Champagne in which red grape skins are permitted slight contact with the

must. Red wine is added to the basic *cuvée.*

26. *La méthode champenoise*

27. The Marne

28. Rhiems

29. The amount of sugar used in making Champagne

30. Each vineyard has its own classification.

31. Racks used to hold the bottles slightly tilted during the second fermentation

32. A bottle actually standing on its head

33. Moët et Chandon

34. Wine (Champagne) made from gentle pressing of the finest grapes, blended with special care to make a wine even better than vintage Champagne

35. Dom Pérignon (Moët et Chandon), 1921

36. "Recently Disgorged"

37. Eight to ten years

38. The original wines from the Champagne region were red and still. The bubbles were thought to be frivolous, and some experts said they spoiled the wine.

GERMANY

1. Southwestern (Palatinate [Rheinpfalz])

2. Rhine, Mosel, Main and Neckar

3. Black or red grapes are difficult to grow in northern latitudes.

4. Wine growing region

5. 11 regions

6. Seven (Ahr, Mittelrhein, Hessische, Nahe, Rheinhessen, Rheingau and Rheinpfalz)

7. Rheingau

8. One

9. Mosel-Saar-Ruwer (three rivers in the area)

10. Peak wines (Rheinhessen wines the most outstanding)

11. Four: (1) Deutcher Tafelwein (table wine); (2) Deutcher Landwein;

(3) Qualitätswein (Qb.A) (quality wine); and (4) Qualitätswein mit Pradikat (QmP) (highest quality)

12. 8.5%. They also must be produced from grapes of a given region.

13. The wine has passed both laboratory and taste tests.

14. Qb.A, region of origin and control number

15. *Erzeugerabfüllung* (bottled by the producer)

16. They must come from a particular district within a region, and "Prädikat" rating depends on the time of the picking and sweetness.

17. 10% (without the addition of sugar during fermentation)

18. In "bad" years, very little (or no) QmP wine will be produced.

19. The addition of sugar to fermenting wine

20. QmP wines may not be *gallized;* Qb.A wines can be, but only under specific circumstances.

21. They are ranked in five categories.

22. Kabinett: picking time, fully matured grapes

23. When they are fully ripe

24. Spätlese: late selected, naturally sweet wine

25. *After* they are ripe

26. For added sweetness

27. Auslese: grapes from selected bunches

28. Beerenauslese: grapes are selected berry by berry.

29. Trockenbeerenauslese: berries are picked as late as December or January and only the very best are selected (overripe, unbroken skins), yielding the greatest wines of Germany.

30. Beerenauslese and Trockenbeerenauslese

31. Made with grapes picked while frozen and crushed before they thaw

32. Only QmP

33. QmP (or Qualitätswein mit Pradikät), the category (e.g., Kabinett), wine region, and control number

34. *Bereich* (district), town and village

35. Area formed by a group of neighboring vineyards

36. 1879

37. *Süss*

38. Dry

39. White wine

40. Sparkling wine made by the traditional *methode champenoise*

41. *Vins du pays*

42. Pfalz (Palatinate)

43. Auction or directly to purchasers through brokers (Friehand sale)

44. Rhine

45. Mosel

46. Wines from Franconia

47. Riesling, Sylvaner and Müller-Thurgau

48. Crossing the Sylvaner and Riesling

49. Palatinate

50. When the wine contains 85% of that grape

51. *Gebiet* (region), *Bereich* (district), *Grosslage* (subdistrict), and *Lage* (vineyard)

52. The sweeter, the more expensive

53. Rheinhessen, Rheinpfalz and Rheingau

54. "Rhenish": at the time it was red

55. "Hock"

56. Ordinary wine

57. Moselblümchen

58. Sweetening agent (grape juice)

59. Term used to describe the Franconian bottle

60. Baden

61. The Egon-Müller family

62. An association which sells some of its wine at auction with extremely high standards; some say that from this association comes the finest German wines.

63. The business center of Moselle, the oldest city in Germany and birthplace of Karl Marx

64. Lower alcoholic content

65. Wine cellar

66. "Bottled by producer"

67. "From the producers own estate"

68. Sparkling wine made from 60% German wine

69. Slightly sparkling wine

70. Pink wine made from red grapes

71. Red wine

72. Low in alcohol

73. Spätburgunder (Pinot Noir) and the Portugieser

74. The valley of the Ahr

75. Trier

76. Bad Kreuznach

77. Passage of The Wine Law, 1971

78. Stuttgart

79. Schloss Böckelheimer Kupfergrube

80. Bernkasteler Doktor

81. Bernkasteler Schwanen and Badstube

82. Zeltingen

83. Palatinate

84. Cafe wine, never bottled unless designated Liebfraumilch

85. Mosel

86. The warm breezes of the Gulf Stream

87. Sylvaner, Müller-Thurgau and Gewürztraminer

88. Quality wine of distinction

89. Müller-Thurgau

90. Blue Nun

91. Liebfraumilch

92. Trier

93. Celts

94.. Südliche Weinstrasse, Mittel Haardt and Oberhaardt

95. The best wines in the Rheinhessen

96. Rheingau

97. Northern most latitude for viticulture

98. Nova Scotia

99. Three (dry, medium dry and mild)

100. 11%

101. Riesling

102. Autumn

103. Balmy October with a late frost

104. Grape-gathering time

105. German wine seal given to wines of especially high quality within their taste delineation (mild, medium dry, dry); this seal appears on the label.

106. German Agricultural Society

107. Celebration for a harvest safely brought in

108. New wine

109. A mixture of Spätburgunder and Burgunder in Baden

110. One of the oldest German wine growing areas, on the western slopes of the
Oldenwald near Heidelberg

111. At the French border

112. Saar

113. Designated quality wine producing
area

114. Palatinate

115. Rheingau

116. Test number of a quality wine

117. Highly perfumed grape

118. A commune

119. Half dry

120. Forst

121. Schloss Johannisberg

122. Winery

123. St. Urban, appropriately enough a
French saint, the bishop of Autun. His
feast day is May 25th.

ITALY

1. Asti Spumante

2. Spumante and Vermouth

3. They produce Spumante and Vermouth.

4. Turin

5. Bianco (white) and Rosato (red)

6. False

7. Three

8. Denominazione di Origine Semplice

9. The broad region

10. Denominazione di Origine Controllata

11. Denominazione Controllata e Garantila (D.O.C.G.)

12. A seal over the cork

13. Cortese

14. Piedmont

15. Coronata, Portofino and Vermentino

16. Cinque Terre

17. Emilia-Romagna

18. The Trebbiano (named for the River Trebbia)

19. Scandiano

20. Lambrusco

21. Albana

22. Tuscany

23. Pinot Noir and Riesling

24. False (it produces both red and white)

25. Umbria

26. Frascati

27. Marino, Grottaferrata and Monteporzio Catone

28. White

29. False (Orvieto is always white)

30. Est! Est!! Est!!!

31. A bishop named Fugger

32. 200

33. "Marchio Nazionale"

34. Valle d'Aosta

35. Donnaz and Enfer d'Arvier

36. Sfursat

37. Soave, Bardolino, Valpolicella

38. Veneto

39. Black, gray and white

40. Cinque Terre and Dolceacqua

41. Lambrusco, Sangiovese di Romagna, Albana di Romagna and Trebbiano di Romagna

42. False

43. Semi-sweet

44. True

45. False

46. Corvo

47. The Tanano

48. A grape

49. The Nebbiolo

50. Chianti

51. Barone Bettino Ricasoli

52. Four

53. The Reservas

54. Biondi-Santi

55. Puglia

56. Vino Passito or Vino Santo

57. True

58. Slightly sparkling

59. *Governo all'usotoscano*

60. During Holy Week ("Vin Santo" means "Holy Wine")

61. Verdicchio

62. 1963

63. Oenotina

64. The Nebbiolo grape

65. Barolo

66. False

67. False — they have nothing to do with each other.

68. Lago di Caldaro

69. Vernaccia

70. White

71. A fiasco

72. True (because of the climate)

73. Bardolino, Valpolicella and Soave

74. Red

75. The Alps

76. Germany

77. Almost 50%

78. Almost 10%

79. A very sweet wine

80. Bottled on the premises of the firm

81. A very light red

82. Wine fun

83. Very old, mellow, ripe wine

84. Cinqueterre

85. Dolceacqua (Rossese)

86. White

87. Yes

88. Very light reds (or very dark rosés)

89. Both are reds

90. Both are reds

91. Lago di Caldaro

92. Procanico

93. False—the wine produced there is Orvieto.

94. Red

95. Red

96. Cannonau and Oliena

97. Sardinia

98. White

99. White

100. Sicily

101. A D.O.C. label

102. False

103. Originates in the town of Asti in Piedmont, and is made from the Muscat grape

104. Antonio Mastroberardino

105. Drink it with pleasure. It is a wine made from the Nebbiolo grape in the Valtellina section of Lombardy.

106. A wine drunk by the ancient Romans

SPAIN/PORTUGAL

1. False — it's third after Italy and France.

2. 1970

3. Rioja

4. The Ebro River

5. Calcareons clay, iron-bearing clay and alluvial salt

6. The Tempranillo

7. A light red wine

8. False — a *reserva* must only be aged six or more years.

9. Wine cellar

10. Ivory

11. The Airén

12. Southern Spain

13. Reds

14. Mostly white wines

15. Málaga

16. The Palomino

17. Jerez de la Frontera or simply "Jerez"

18. True

19. Albariza

20. Jerez or Jerez de la Frontera

21. Fino, Oloroso and Palo Cortado

22. *Flor*

23. Manzanilla

24. A fortified Fino wine (15-16%)

25. A more fortified Fino wine (18%)

26. Palo Cortado

27. A vintage wine

28. The *solera* system

29. Criaderas, or "cradles"

30. No, because most are blends of different *soleras*

31. No

32. 17-22%

33. Port

34. Reds predominate

35. More whites (and also rosés)

36. Six

37. Denominaçâo de Origen

38. Green wines

39. For their youth

40. Minho, Dâo, Setúbal, Bucelas, Carcavelos and Colares

41. False — it produces and exports white wines.

42. Port

43. Port can be both red and white.

44. True

45. True

46. False — it's unlikely to reach maturity before it's twenty years old.

47. The crust

48. Tawny, ruby and white

49. To the Instituto de Vinho de Ports

50. The Spanish word for flower, it refers to an unusual and special yeast native to the Sherry area of Spain.

51. A type of Sherry: generally the palest, dryest and most delicate

52. While he served at Fort Independence in Boston Harbor

53. A *criadera* is the place in a Spanish *bodega* where the young wines are cared for; the word means "nursery" in Spanish.

54. Jerez, Rioja and Penedes

55. Angelica, named for the city of Los Angeles

56. The agricultural estates in Portugal where the grapes used in making Port wine are grown

57. A Port wine that gains its tawny color from long years of aging in wood

58. A blended Port that may contain as many as 30 different Ports, aged using the *solera* system

59. A Vintage Port is Port wine declared so by the winemakers because the particular year was exceptional. Not every year is a vintage year. Vintage Port is aged two to three years in the barrel before bottling.

60. Champagne or *vin mousseaux*

61. A grape used in making Port

62. A thin film or crust which forms in some old bottled Port

GRAPES

1. Basic element found in red wine skins that aids in aging

2. Gives the wine character and ability to age

3. Seeds, stem and stalk

4. Skins are removed before fermentation

5. Sherry

6. Study of wines

7. Riesling

8. Grape farming

9. Wine making

10. Wax-like surface of the grape

11. Yeast

12. Aids in fermentation by breaking down the grape sugars

13. Blanc Fumé

14. Châteauneuf-du-Pape

15. Sicilian white wines

16. Veneto

17. Bardolino and Valpolicella

18. Dry white wines of Franken

19. Pineau d'Aunis

20. Chenin Blanc

21. New York State

22. Red, full, soft — sometimes called Maréchal Foch

23. New York State

24. Sparkling wines

25. Native sweet wines

26. Dry white wines (U.S.)

27. Sweet dessert wines

28. White and sparkling wines

29. New York State

30. Sparkling wines

31. Zinfandel

32. Sweetened kosher red wines

33. Flowery white wines

34. Duriff

35. Soft, red California wines

36. Blending and California reds

37. Varietals, and some blending

38. Sharp, fruity white wines

39. Used for varietals; almost the same as used in French Beaujolais

40. Generics, mostly blending

41. Chardonnay

42. Gamay formed wine; Chardonnay for white

43. Chardonnay

44. Roussette

45. Mauyac

46. Grenache

47. Muscadet

48. Portugese black grape used for making Port

49. Muscadelle and White Riesling

50. Italian white grape

51. Tannin, coloring

52. Merlot

53. Warm, dry regions of southern France

54. Bandol wines

55. Grenache

56. Six

57. One (Gamay)

58. Blanc de Blanc

59. Grape harvest

60. Pinot Noir

61. Alsace

62. Riesling

63. Sauvignon blanc

64. Fumé Blanc

65. Pouilly Fumé

66. Cabernet Franc

67. Pinot Noir

68. Burgandies

69. Cabernet Sauvignon

70. Pinot Blanc and Pinot Gris

71. Noble rot

72. Sémillon

73. Sweet white wines (i.e., Sauternes, Barsac and Laupiac)

74. Chardonnay

75. Chardonnay

76. Spicy

77. Sauvignon Rosé

78. Chenin Blanc

79. Riesling

PEOPLE, PLACES AND THINGS

Answers to Pictures

Picture 1

The Shafers (John R., Julie, Libby, Doug and Bett) of Shafer Vineyards, a small yet prestigious family owned and operated winery in the Napa Valley, producers of Cabernet, Chardonnay and Merlot.

Picture 2

Three prominent figures of the California wine industry: Sam Sebastiani, William Hill and Michael Mondavi (of Sebastiani, Hill, and Mondavi Wineries) — here, they are displaying the 1985 Presidential Inauguration Commemorative Wines.

Picture 3

Castello Banfi — the latest acquisition of Villa Banfi (U.S.A.). This castle dates back to 800 A.D. and overlooks the firm's 7,100-acre vineyard estate and new winery in Montalcino, Italy.

Picture 4

Grape harvest in 1871 (Buena Vista Winery) in Sonoma, California. Note the curved pruning knife (held by the man on the left), which is the same used today. In the background can be seen Agoston Haraszthy's villa, which was later destroyed by fire. The "press house," built in 1862 and originally used for storing caves and cellars, now is used for tours and as a tasting room.

Picture 5

Count Agoston Haraszthy, Father of American Viticulture

Picture 6

The Pavilion of the Buena Vista Vinicultural Society — Vienna Exhibition, 1873

Picture 7

Andre Gagey, Managing Director for Maison Louis Jadot

Picture 8

Philippe Court, Managing Director for Champagne Taittinger

Picture 9

Brother Timothy, F.S.C., Cellarmaster of Christian Brothers, owner of perhaps the finest collection of corkscrews in the world. Here, he is using the "F.E. Walton Cork Drawer."

Picture 10

Brother Timothy's five best corkscrews

a. "Hallmarked Silver Swan," Netherlands, 1800

b. "Large boar tusk/silver eagle," U.S.A., 1900

c. "Mother of pearl, barrel-shape," France, 1750

d. "Hallmarked silver nutmeg grater," England, 1805

e. "Gentleman's silver," Germany, 1897